THE RACING STABLE

MARCEL METZE

THE
RACING
STABLE

The Dedicated, Assertive, Adaptive
Journey of The Member Company

Warden Press

© 2021 Marcel Metze

ISBN 978-94-93202-00-9 (paperback)
ISBN 978-94-93202-02-3 (hardcover)
ISBN 978-94-93202-03-0 (e-book)

Interior design: Sander Pinkse Boekproductie, Amsterdam
Cover design and artwork: Studio Brand, The Hague

wardenpress.com

TABLE OF CONTENTS

COMPASS

HOW TO READ THIS BOOK

This is a book about a high-tech and R&D consultancy based in the high-tech heart of the Netherlands. It's also a book about the world in which this company and its people are living: a futuristic world, filled with technologies that make you feel as if you're in a science fiction movie. And that's still not all because it's also a book about professional and personal development, about setbacks and successes, about how to survive crises, about finding one's way in volatile and uncertain times.

The title, *The Racing Stable,* can only refer to the people who are central to The Member Company: its employeneurs — a term TMC invented to characterize its people, not as staff, personnel or hired hands but as proud and independent entrepreneurial employees. Indeed, the ones I've encountered are all highly qualified engineers, fundamentally optimistic, forward looking, result oriented, fascinated by their projects, determined to give their best to the clients they're working for, while at the same time eager to get the best out of themselves. You can meet them too, if you continue reading.

A ROADMAP

Being the author, I of course hope you will read this book from beginning to end. But I'm realistic. People are busy and have different interests. For that reason I have prepared a roadmap, with a variety of routes through the book, tailored to the different target groups it wants to reach. So...

Target group		**Chapters**
Deep Divers	⟶	entire book
Graduate Student or recently graduated engineer	⟶	introduction 3 and 4
Experienced Engineer	⟶	3, 4, 5 and 6
High-tech company executive	⟶	1 and 6
Student or teacher in business administration	⟶	1, 2, 3, 5 and 7
HR-manager, assessment expert or coach	⟶	3, 4 and 6

If you want to take a deep dive into the TMC world…

… meet the group's entrepreneurial engineers, learn about the futuristic projects they are working on, are interested in professional and personal development, and find out what it's like to build a hundred-million-euro company and guide it through three global crises, read: the entire book.

If you're a graduate student or recently graduated engineer…

… and want to know how TMC welcomes its newbies, and what kind of projects TMC engineers are working on, you should certainly read: introduction, chapter 3, chapter 4.

What is your desire? (the introduction) offers you a first look at TMC and the way the company welcomes its new employeneurs.

In *Transparency, that's the disruptive thing* (chapter 3) you will meet experienced and new employeneurs, take a deeper look inside the model and get an impression of TMC's internal social systems and support tools.

After that, you may also want to take a look at the section "The pursuit of happiness" in chapter 4 (*The pilots*) and read how Ignacio

Vazquez started to work for TMC. And don't forget to take a peek at the pages about the fantastic technologies that are being co-developed by TMC's engineers in chapter 6 (*The client*) and about the Belgian, French and Swedish experiences in chapter 5 (*Going abroad*).

If you are an experienced engineer...

... and want to know what it's like to work as a TMC employeneur on projects at high-tech and R&D companies on the frontline of Industry 4.0, you can read: chapters 3, 4, 5 and 6.

In *Transparency, that's the disruptive thing* (chapter 3) you will meet colleagues and learn about the financial stability, transparency, individual profit sharing and entrepreneurial opportunities TMC offers. Once you're done with that, you might meet more colleagues in the four Tech Talk paragraphs in chapter 4 (*The pilots*); read about TMC Belgium, France and Sweden in chapter 5 (*Going abroad*); and find examples of projects at client companies (chapter 6, *The client*).

If you are a high-tech company executive...

...and want to know more about TMC and its people, you could begin by reading: chapters 1 and 6.

Start small, think big (chapter 1) describes TMC's roots, its basic philosophy and its first years.

The client (chapter 6) describes client experiences, which will obviously be interesting for you, as will *Going abroad* (chapter 5), which details TMC's international expansion strategy since 2014; and *Transparency, that's the disruptive thing* (chapter 3), in which you will find out more about TMC's specializations.

If you are a student or teacher in business administration...

...or a business historian, you should definitely read:
- in chapter 1:
  - "Into the core," about the start of TMC
  - "Fifteen percent, minus that is...," about the dot.com crisis and 9/11
- in chapter 2:
  - "What is your key technology," about the group's expansion in the Netherlands in 2005–2007
  - "Eckart Wintzen upgraded" about how TMC took business cells to the next level

- – "Going too fast," how TMC handled a failed takeover and the 2008–2009 credit crisis
- – "The buy-out," how TMC left the stock exchange
- in chapter 3:
  - – "TMC's business cells: continuity, innovation and expansion," about TMC's specializations and expansion strategy
- in chapter 5:
  - – "A real innovation," about TMC's international expansion strategy since 2014
- in chapter 7:
  - – how TMC handled the early months of the Covid-19 crisis

If you are an HR manager, assessment expert or coach...
... I advise you to read: chapters 3, 4 and 6.
In chapter 3, *Transparency, that's the disruptive thing,* you could focus on pillar 4: YOUniversity, about TMC's personal and professional development tools.
Chapter 4, *The pilots,* will probably interest you from beginning to end, since it explains the employeneur analysis and its underlying tests, describes the role of coaching in TMC, and offers stories of employeneurs about their experiences with coaching. The chapter also takes you inside employeneurship theory and the foundations of the employeneurship construct.
In chapter 6, *The client*, you might be interested to read about the "conversion problem" and about the developments in the high-tech consultancy business in the last decade.

Enjoy and learn!

Marcel Metze
September 2020

INTRODUCTION

WHAT IS YOUR DESIRE?

———

TMC – ALL ABOUT YOU

It's 8:30 in the morning, December 6, 2019. TMC's four-story headquarters is a modest building. It stands in the corner of an open field, next to a similar building, occupied by another company. From a distance, both bear a faint resemblance to Rubik's Cubes, with clear glass panes instead of the colored squares of the 3D puzzle. The field is part of the High Tech Campus on the edge of Eindhoven, an industrial town in the southern province of North Brabant, the Netherlands. Dozens of technological companies have settled on the campus' 250 acres. This particular field is its most recent extension. It offers plenty of space for many more buildings to come, and on one of its edges a brand new parking garage lies waiting, hidden behind an earthen barrier that shields the campus from the noisy A2 highway.

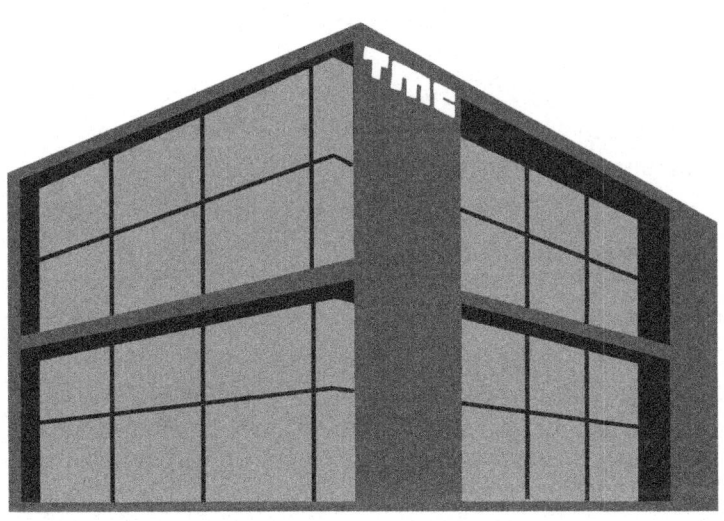

It is winter; at this hour the day is still dawning. Sixteen people, all engineers, gather in a room on the second floor — a standard conference room with white tables arranged in a U shape, a huge LCD screen on one of the white walls, and white light shining down from a white-squared ceiling. Thirteen men, three women, some young, others already showing traces of gray, all casually dressed. They're silent, maybe not quite awake yet, maybe a bit shy — it's the first time they've met and, let's be frank, engineers are not known for their social skills.

Their host is 39-year-old Sven Bongartz, manager of TMC Mechanical, one of the company's business cells. He too is still in low gear. A few minutes into his presentation he realizes he hasn't introduced himself. He apologizes: "My girlfriend and I have a three-year-old daughter and our son was born three weeks ago. So if you think, 'he looks tired,' you're right."

Then he speeds up. Using a somewhat worn-out pun he explains the TMC acronym: no, it does not refer to Thijs Manders, the man who founded the company twenty years ago. It's short for The Member Company. Because "TMC is all about *you*. It's a vehicle for *your* development, and *you* are at the wheel."

To the outsider, these sentences might sound as if Sven took them straight from a recruiting brochure. Yet, this is what TMC deeply believes. The company wants to treat its highly skilled engineers as both employees and entrepreneurs: *employeneurs* in TMC lingo. There are around a thousand of them on its payroll at the time of writing. They don't work for TMC, TMC works for them. The company sends them to a wide variety of high-tech firms in the Netherlands, Belgium, France and, increasingly, other European countries. There, they contribute to projects, mostly in research and development or production innovation, lasting from one to several years. To help them self-manage their careers and career paths, TMC offers them an array of tools and benefits such as individual profit sharing, personal coaching, a YOUniversity to continue their professional development and an Entrepreneurial Lab for those who want to start a business of their own. At the same time, TMC tries to be a home base by providing them the financial security of permanent contracts and the professional warmth of business cells, where they can meet colleagues who speak their technical language and with whom they can share experiences and ideas. Together, the permanent contracts, the individual profit sharing, the YOUniversity, the lab and the business cells constitute TMC's five core principles.

So TMC may be "all about you" — as Sven Bongartz says to the sixteen newbies — but it also wants to be a social environment with shared values and elements of a family culture. In its corporate philosophy, the company celebrates both individualism and inclusion, a seemingly paradoxical combination that, until recently, around the turn of the millennium, could only have been dreamed of.

Then there's music. The new employeneurs — themselves probably not yet used to the term — are invited to dance a bit and then, as soon as the music stops, ask the person closest to them about his or her background. The atmosphere in the room becomes more lively now. Once they have retaken their seats — the tables now set in a square — the introductions continue. One by one, the participants explain who they are and why they have chosen TMC as their professional base. Data scientist Nithin: "I wanted to start an independent practice, but I didn't have the necessary skills." Nicole says she experiences regular jobs "as a prison" and wants "to develop my entrepreneurial side." Laura obtained her master's degree in nanotechnology just four months ago. She describes herself as "very inquisitive," and finds TMC appealing because she doesn't want to spend her entire working life at one company. She wants to eventually start her own business.

The group descends to the ground floor for a short visit to TMC's Entrepreneurial Lab — an L-shaped space filled with high-tech tools and equipment. They are welcomed by Steven Verboom, one of TMC's more experienced employeneurs. Steven describes the lab as a "playroom" for engineers. He points to a wheelchair in a corner: a soccer robot for handicapped children. Using a mechanism attached to its footrest, the children can both kick and catch a ball. Another lab team is working on a Throwabot, a small robot that can be thrown into a building or onto a ship (from another ship) to check for dangerous explosives. The Dutch Ministry of Defense is interested. "Many people have ideas for new products," Sven continues, "but at their workplace, they usually won't get the time and budget to develop them." So TMC offers them that possibility. Steven's enthusiasm about The Entrepreneurial Lab knows no bounds: "This is a place where revolutionary ideas are born. It's the superlative of employeneurship. And if you succeed in bringing your invention to market, you will keep your intellectual ownership."

When the sixteen new employeneurs return from a lunch break, they find the tables in the conference room in yet another arrangement: joined in sets of two, with four chairs around them. A new host takes over: Loek Ghering, manager of TMC's YOUniversity. He shows a video "that always makes me silent and reflective": *what is your desire?* It's a dreamy film, full of romantic images and gentle music. A warm male voice asks, "What would you like to do if money was no object?" and basically repeats one message: it's stupid to spend your life doing things you don't like. It turns out that the voice belongs to Alan Watts (1915–1973), a British philosopher and Zen Buddhist who lived in California and attracted a large following in the 1960s. Watts wrote many books and articles about Zen Buddhism and what we now call mindfulness, and was a firm believer in the richness of human potential. Judging by their popularity on YouTube, the lectures of this hippie guru still find a large audience — his "if money was no object" speech has been watched/listened to almost four million times on the site.[1]

In one of his early works, entitled *The Wisdom of Insecurity*, Watts discussed man's search for stability in vulnerable and uncertain times. His own frame of reference was World War II and the Cold War (he published the book in 1951), during which vulnerability and uncertainty reached their depths. Yet, seven decades later, people in our own prosperous and relatively peaceful Western world might well use these same words to describe their own age, albeit for different reasons than fear of war. In fact, insecurity is a key element in the so-called VUCA model. This world-view came into being in the late 1980s, when the end of the Cold War and the rise of China opened up the perspective of tectonic shifts in the existing geopolitical relations, and became increasingly popular in strategic leadership theories at the beginning of the new millennium. Today's reality, the VUCA model says, is *volatile, uncertain, complex* and *ambiguous*. We may lament that, but somehow we have to deal with it. Not by hiding in a corner but by going out into the world and embracing it as it is. One of Alan Watts' key concepts was adaptability. As he wrote, "The art of living in this [...] 'predicament' is neither careless drifting on the one hand nor fearful clinging to the past and the known on the other. It consists in being completely sensitive to each moment, in regarding it as utterly new and unique, in having the mind open and wholly receptive."[2]

The art of living in a VUCA world also requires, one should add, getting to know yourself and the ability to shape your own course in life — in TMC lingo: to plot your own *Yourney*. As TMC's theoretician Freek van Bedaf — himself a staunch adherent to the VUCA worldview — likes to say, "It's all about your self-propelling capacity." We'll meet Van Bedaf more in-depth later in this book. He has spent several decades analyzing and measuring this self-propelling capacity, which he finally decided would be best described as executional intelligence, or XQ. We're not talking about a marketing label here, mind you. Underneath it lies a philosophy of identity and personality that is akin to the ideas of the famous American sociologist Richard Sennett, who has written many books and essays about flexible labor and its effects on career development, professional identity and the development of a coherent personality. That's serious stuff.

What is your desire? After showing the Allan Watts video, TMC's YOUniversity manager Loek Ghering invites the sixteen newly hired employeneurs to discuss that question and summarize their answers on a whiteboard. Most describe their desires in cautious and abstract terms: "development," "a goal," "balance," "humor." Only one divulges a secret dream: "I'd like to build a warp portal and go to space." Ghering, sensing that the group doesn't know how to react to this frankness, gently warns: "You *can* get lost in freedom." It seems as good a moment as any to introduce the external coaches who are at each employeneur's disposal. Ghering encourages the newbies to fill out the Employeneur Analysis, which was developed by Freek van Bedaf. The results will show the strengths and weaknesses in their XQ and will be a good starting point for a first coaching session. Ghering: "You get seven sessions per year, and more if necessary. Do it. You can discuss anything with your coach. That may feel uncomfortable at first, but everything you say will remain confidential."

***

So this is how TMC welcomes its new members. Some readers may wonder why this welcome mainly seems to focus on their soft skills. The answer is both simple and complex. The simple part is that their hard skills don't need much attention. In their technical fields, they belong to the best and brightest. It's their soft skills that need nurturing for them to thrive in the efficiency-driven and sometimes

very stressful industrial environments in which they will develop or continue their careers. They must be able to work in teams, communicate with non-technicians, manage, supervise, build a professional network, acquire a strategic vision on their career development, et cetera, et cetera. The complex part is to actually do all this in a conscious, mindful way when, in practice, the daily routines of life and work usually allow very little time and space for things like getting to know yourself, improving your soft skills and developing your personality.

TMC sees finding talented engineers and nurturing the balance between their hard and soft skills as the core of its business model. It's a philosophy that has paid off. The group was incorporated in the year 2000. By the end of 2019, it operated from eighteen offices in ten countries, had a turnover of €103 million, realized just over €13 million in earnings (EBITDA)[3] and was ready to expand its already ambitious program of internationalization.

Are you curious to find out how they did this?
Then read on.

CHAPTER 1

START SMALL, THINK BIG

—

THE CITY OF LIGHT

It is no coincidence that TMC originated in the Eindhoven region. The southern Dutch city is the product of high-tech dreams. In the late 19th century it was hardly more than a village, surrounded by vast moorlands and situated far from the major Dutch and Flemish urban centers. Its less than five thousand inhabitants worked the neighboring fields; its small-scale mills produced textiles, cigars and leather goods. The local elite consisted of landholders, factory owners and the Catholic clergy. Then, in 1891, on the brink of the 20th century, Gerard Philips, an electrical engineer, arrived. Using money from his father — a well-to-do banker — he bought an abandoned weaving mill and, building on technology he had picked up in Scotland and England, began producing incandescent lightbulbs. Four years later he was joined by his younger brother Anton, who turned out to be a sales genius. Together, Gerard and Anton Philips laid the foundations for an electrical engineering/electronics conglomerate which, at its peak, employed up to 400,000 people worldwide. The Physics Laboratory they started in 1914 soon began to produce a steady stream of inventions and innovations, and today still is a core institution — now called Philips Research — on Eindhoven's High Tech Campus. TMC's headquarters are just a stone's throw down the road.

Anton and Gerard didn't just build a corporate empire, they also drove the expansion of Eindhoven into a City of Light and a true Philips Town, with over a hundred thousand inhabitants by the mid-1930s, Philips schools, Philips medical services, Philips housing quarters, Philips sports facilities, a Philips soccer club (today still called PSV, short for Philips Sport Vereniging), a Philips cultural center, and thousands and thousands of Philips employees. Since the mid-1970s the company has withdrawn from its role as a public services provider and divested many of its non-core (and ultimately even core) activities. Today Eindhoven has a quarter of a million inhabitants. It no longer is Philips Town but one might call it, with good reason, Philips Spin-Off Town. As the Philips Group retreated in the 1980s and 1990s, closed factories, sold subsidiaries and moved its headquarters to Amsterdam, in the Eindhoven region dozens of ICT start-ups, specialized electronic hardware and components producers, consulting and services companies and new high-tech giants sprang up. The most well-known no doubt are ASML — the worldwide number one producer of photolithography systems for the computer chip industry — and chip producer NXP Semiconductors. And of course Royal Philips, now focusing on medical systems (mainly diagnostic imaging equipment), maintains a significant presence.

Thijs Manders (December 7, 1963) was born and raised in this region, and so was his neighbor and boyhood friend Hans Strieder (1965). Their mothers were friends, both their fathers worked for Royal Philips — then still called Royal Philips' Incandescent Lamp Works. When I interviewed Strieder in early 2019, he was working at ASML Group, where he is the global human resources business partner for manufacturing, with sites in the Netherlands, the US and Asia. "I see Thijs as my brother," he said, "even though we are very different. I always have both feet on the ground; Thijs has the ability to take me to the air." Two decades ago, he helped Thijs set up TMC. He fondly recalled his first days. "They had a nice office, beautiful chairs and impressive business cards, but their purse was empty. Typical Thijs. He likes to think big."[1]

When I told Manders about Strieder's recollection, during an interview in January 2020, he smiled. "Our purse was empty? It wasn't as bad as that." He took an additional mortgage on his house, which had increased in value in the preceding years, and found a major co-investor in Jan van Rijt, who ran an accountancy and fiscal consultancy firm and had earlier set up an ICT services company. "We had half a million guilders plus a bank credit line of another half million, so a million in total." And as far as big spending was concerned: during the first five years, TMC occupied modest offices at Van Rijt's firm in Rosmalen, a village near the city of Den Bosch, some forty kilometers north of Eindhoven.[2]

When he and Van Rijt founded the company, in February 2000, Manders had just turned thirty-six. After high school, he had trained as a personnel manager at Eindhoven's Social Academy; his friend Strieder went there as well, some years later. The political climate at these academies was rather liberal. They offered courses in social work, community building and personnel management. But the personnel managers who graduated from them tended to think like trade union representatives. "I didn't like it at all," Manders said. "Leftist atmosphere, people were still smoking marijuana." He stayed, nevertheless, and took an interest in sociology, psychology, and issues like power and ethics in labor relations.[3]

His first student internship was in 1985 at PTT Post, then still a state-owned postal service. That too was an educational experience. "They had far too many people in the personnel department, who started work with a half-hour coffee session and went home at 4:30 pm." But time was on his side. In the mid-1980s, many Dutch companies in manufacturing and finance set out on an automation drive. This resulted in an explosion of computer start-ups, in hardware, software and services. In 1987, Manders found a job at Tulip Computers, a new PC manufacturer. That was a totally different experience. "Everybody wore business suits, and I learned to work very hard." A year later Tulip appointed him, at the age of 25, as their personnel manager. "I think I was the youngest personnel manager in the Netherlands." Three years later, he moved to the recruitment services sector. First he was hired by EGOR, a French consultancy that was dissolved in 1993, then moved to a recruitment company in The Hague. In 1996, he wound up at Young Executive Recruitment (YER), a then eight-year-old Dutch firm, which put him in charge of setting up an Eindhoven office. In those days, most recruiting firms focused on finding financial experts. But after contacting tech companies like Philips, Ericsson, Océ van der Grinten (a printer producer) and ASML, Manders quickly found that they were yearning for engineers in the Eindhoven region. "ASML had a thousand job openings in those days." So he began recruiting non-optical lithography experts and software engineers.[4]

He found out some other things as well. Because of the tight labor market, computer and software service bureaus had no problem placing their experts, and they put little effort into building durable relationships with their clients. "The clients said: after they send us someone, we hardly see them anymore. And if we then want to hire the expert on a permanent basis, that's impossible due to competition clauses." In addition, both the clients and the experts complained about a lack of transparency about the percentage of the fees the service bureaus pocketed.[5]

▌ INTO THE CORE

It turns out that Manders did initially derive the name of his new company from his own name. "Three-letter company names were popular in the ICT world, so TMC fitted nicely." He kept the acronym, but soon decided that The Member Company as underlying name would better reflect his intentions, which were, from the very start, "To offer my engineers a permanent contract and an individual share in my company's profits, to invest in their personal and professional development, and to build a relationship with the clients we sent them to."[6]

That he was thinking big is evident. Right from the start, he shaped TMC as a holding company with three subsidiaries. The first to become operational was TMC Embedded Software, a consultancy for the deployment of software engineers, run by Geert Eijkhout, who joined the club in March 2000. In April, Freek van Bedaf joined as well. Freek had trained as a lawyer and management expert. In jobs at the Dutch National Immigration & Naturalization Service and with Hays, the recruitment group, he had developed an interest in assessment and training methods. In 1999, Thijs Manders asked him to set up TMC Assessment & Development, the subsidiary that would offer assessment and coaching services. Finally, in October, Hans Strieder came in to run the third subsidiary, TMC Executive Recruitment.[7]

By that time, Manders had found his main concept. "On the 13th of July, a hot day, it simply dropped into my head: our people aren't *werknemers* [employees], they aren't *ondernemers* [entrepreneurs], they are *werk/ondernemers*. Employeneurs."

As Hans Strieder pointed out, the new company also quickly developed its strategic vision. When I met him in early 2019 in his ASML office, he took a piece of paper and drew three concentric circles. "This is how high-tech companies build their workforce," he explained. "The outer circle is a flexible layer of well-trained, skilled people, mostly working in production. The middle layer consists of highly trained, highly skilled employees, partly on fixed contracts, partly hired on a temporary basis, mainly in managerial and developmental roles. Then there is the core, consisting of people who are top-level experts in their field and who are crucial for the development and innovation of the company's core technologies." What TMC wanted to do, was to find the best and the brightest engineers and "send them into their clients' technological core."[8]

top-level experts

Highly trained, highly skilled

Well-trained, skilled people

TMC

Unfortunately, while TMC was getting off the ground, external circumstances were deteriorating quickly. Just one month after the company was established, the 1990s dot-com bubble burst. On March 10, 2000, the American Nasdaq Composite Stock Market Index, which included numerous Internet-based companies, reached its peak. During the preceding five years, it had grown fivefold. In the last of those years, it had more than doubled. In 1999, especially, many Internet stock introductions had been outright hypes, with stock prices sometimes rising over 400 percent on the first day of trading, even though the — often very young — companies involved had never shown a profit. Now, triggered by a series of factors (rising inflation and interest rates in the USA, a recession in Japan) the bubble began to collapse. On March 15, merger talks between web services provider Yahoo and e-commerce platform eBay ended without a result, causing the Nasdaq index to drop 2.6 percent. A next significant event was the initial public offering (IPO) of the Dutch Internet service provider World Online on 17 March. The company was valued at €12 billion, even though its 2009 losses (€91 million) had exceeded its revenues (€64 million). The banks issuing the stock put a lot of effort into preventing the price from sinking below its introduction level, but in the post-IPO days, this happened anyway. Within two weeks, World Online's value plunged to €5 billion. On March 20, the influential American financial paper Barron's featured an article which stated that Internet companies were running out of cash fast and predicted that many of them would go bankrupt. On April 3, an American court ruling that Microsoft had violated US antitrust laws led to another fall of the Nasdaq stock index, now by 25 percent in about ten days. In the following months, investors started withdrawing their money from the Internet and high-technology sector; companies in that sector began to scale back their spending and to lay off staff, and — just as Barron's had predicted — an increasing number of them went bankrupt or were acquired by more powerful sister companies.[9]

Surprisingly, TMC wasn't hurt. "We had a very fast start," Manders reminisced during an interview in early 2020, in the office of his investment company, which is located in an old, renovated mansion on the market square of Waalre, the village south of Eindhoven where he lives. "By the end of 2000, we employed fifteen software engineers, five consultants and another five psychologists." In the Netherlands, demand for software engineers, in particular, remained very high. Strieder: "Hourly fees could run as high as four hundred euro's, bonuses in extreme cases up to a hundred thousand."[10]

FIFTEEN PERCENT — MINUS, THAT IS

Despite the dot-com collapse, TMC's growth accelerated in 2001, especially in its Embedded Software division — the software engineering branch — which expanded to around forty people. Then 9/11 came. The terrorist attack on New York City's Twin Towers on the morning of September 11 cost almost three thousand lives and caused billions of dollars in damage. It had an immediate effect on worldwide stock prices, which dropped steeply (the Dow Jones lost around fourteen percent), and on the New York economy. Over four hundred thousand jobs were lost in the city's financial sector in just three months' time, and tens of thousands of jobs more at small businesses like restaurants and lunch places in Lower Manhattan. Worldwide, airline companies and the tourism industry suffered a decrease in travel demand. Moreover, within a month of 9/11, on October 7, the USA invaded Afghanistan and started a war against the Taliban regime, which it suspected of giving shelter to the militant Islamist al-Qaeda movement, which was responsible for the Twin Tower attack.[11]

Despite this distress, the world economy did not seem extremely affected ,and within a few months stock prices started to rebound. The USA fell into a short recession, but that already ended by early 2002. In Europe, the economic situation remained more volatile, due to a weak euro — which had been introduced just three years earlier, in 1999 — and a slow recovery in France and Germany. In addition, the collapse of the dot-com bubble, which had started in March 2000, wasn't over yet, as was illustrated by an accounting scandal at one of the largest US telecommunications businesses, WorldCom, in the spring of 2002, and its bankruptcy in July of that year.[12]

"At first, we didn't notice any effects of 9/11 on our business," Thijs Manders said, looking back from two decades later. "We closed

2001 with a workforce of forty software engineers and fifteen consultants, and a turnover of ten million guilders. But then, in early 2002, everything ground to a halt. Some of my people landed 'on the bench,' as we call it. Not too many, around six, but nevertheless." That wasn't all, though. "The biggest problem was that Philips and other major clients all demanded that we reduce our fees by fifteen percent."[13]

It was TMC's first crisis. Manders: "We had to find a way to survive this." He, typically, didn't choose a defensive but rather a partly offensive, partly adaptive approach. To strengthen the group's finances, he asked his three division managers to make a deposit on the fifteen percent shareholding they had been given in their own subsidiaries. Strieder and Van Bedaf did so. Geert Eijkhout of TMC's Embedded Software branch, on the other hand, preferred to leave the company. Manders: "He bought a Harley Davidson and went on a long voyage. Later, he became very successful, but as far as I know, he still regrets leaving TMC at such an early stage."

The crisis primarily hit TMC's Executive Recruitment branch. By the end of 2002, its manager, Hans Strieder, was spending so much time twiddling his thumbs that he decided to hire himself out as a human resources manager at a software house. "When they offered to pay me a fee of eight hundred euros per day, Thijs suggested I ask for a thousand." He smiled at the memory. Later, in 2003, Strieder was asked to join Assembléon, formerly known as Philips EMT. This was part of Royal Philips Corporate Investment, with a mission to divest a number of smaller subsidiaries which the Royal Philips group wanted to put on their own feet. He said yes and left TMC, as he himself stressed, without any negative feelings. He and Thijs Manders remained friends. Manders restructured TMC's Executive Recruitment division into a TMC SAP, a subsidiary for the deployment of engineers with expertise in implementing the enterprise resource planning (ERP) systems developed by the German software company SAP. Initially, Royal Philips became TMC SAP's main client. Later, the subsidiary's manager, Robert Smits, managed to expand its client base and boost the number of deployed engineers from around ten/twenty at the outset to forty/fifty (TMC SAP was ultimately dismantled in 2008).[14]

According to Thijs Manders, the main reason the 2002 crisis didn't cause TMC very severe damage was that the company maintained its focus on the quality of its engineers. "The employeneurship model began to resonate. We were able to find the best people, and because of that, managed to get increasingly better fees." Growth continued and — little by little — TMC began to recoup the 2002 fee reduction. The golden pre-9/11 days were over, though. "The fees never returned to those levels."[15]

Then, in 2004, he decided it was time for the next step forward.

CHAPTER 2

THE RACING STABLE

"WHAT IS YOUR KEY TECHNOLOGY?"

Jan Mengelers met Thijs Manders in the early 2000s. At the time, Mengelers was the executive director of TNO Industry and Technology, which was one of the focus areas of TNO, the Netherlands Organization for Applied Scientific Research. Today, this institute, founded by law in 1932, has just under three thousand employees and annual income of around €500 million, forty percent of which is provided by the Dutch government. In the early 00s it was considerably larger (five thousand employees). Too large, the government felt, and on top of that too bureaucratic and too inefficient. Its focus on the needs of industry and the market was generally regarded as weak. Based on the conclusions of an external advisory committee, chaired by Herman Wijffels, an economist and former banker, TNO was reorganized in 2005. Its fifteen divisions were regrouped into five focus areas, each subdivided into a series of business units. One of these new focus areas was Jan Mengelers' TNO Industry and Technology.[1]

To work more efficiently and in a project-based way, Mengelers replaced part of his fixed staff with a flexible layer of engineers. TMC was one of the consultancies he hired them from. When I interviewed Mengelers in 2019, he had been chairman of the board of Eindhoven University of Technology for five years. He had left TNO in 2014, but vividly remembered how Manders operated back around 2004–2005. We were sitting in his office on the first floor of the university's central building, which is set on concrete stilts and has glass walls, overlooking the park-like campus. "Initially, I saw TMC as just another secondment bureau," Mengelers said. "But over time it began to strike me that Thijs managed to assemble excellent technicians in his racing stable. He was not a price fighter, but he sent me very good people."[2]

What also struck Mengelers: "Thijs wanted to build and maintain a relationship with us as a client. He always asked me: what is your key technology? And then he began to 'eat' himself into that."[3]

What Mengelers noticed was, in fact, that TMC began to expand its own "focus areas," which it labeled business cells. In 2004, the company's structure was basically still the same as at the start: it had two divisions. After Hans Strieder's departure in 2002, the TMC Executive

Cell Expansion Program

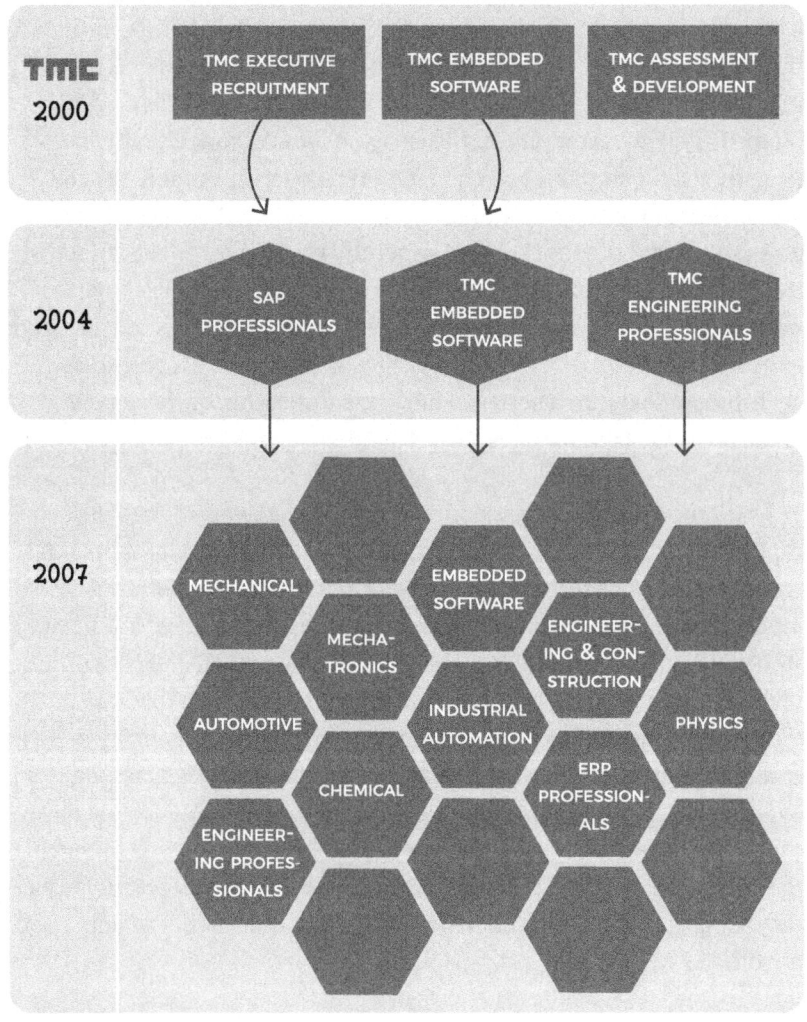

Recruitment division had been transformed into TMC SAP Professionals and focused on ERP (enterprise resource planning software) consultancy. It was managed by Robert Smits, who had joined the company in 2001. At the second division, TMC Embedded Software, Geert Eijkhout left in 2003 and was replaced by Roel Hintzen, who had been with TMC almost from the start.[4]

The cell expansion program began in 2004. That year, Manders hired Roy Roosen, a human resources manager at ASML, and Luuk Jeuken, a recruitment consultant at YER, and tasked them with setting up a third cell: Engineering Professionals. They were made partners and on top of that shareholders of their respective business cells.[5]

In 2005, TMC moved to the Green Tower, an office building in the center of Eindhoven, located on the Vestdijk, with a wide view over the city. "It was our nicest location," Manders fondly remembered during a conversation fifteen years later. "We were on the eleventh floor. The ground floor was occupied by a bar called The Movies, where we did many of our pizza sessions. I think we provided them half of their turnover."[6]

TMC now stepped up the pace. It hired Sander Lieftink to help shape TMC Field Service, an area of expertise which would later evolve into a full-blown cell (Lieftink stayed twelve years at TMC and ultimately became the chief customer officer of TMC Netherlands). From 2005 onwards, the number of cells grew quickly. Discussion with TNO — and specifically with their HR director Wil Janssen — resulted in a chemical cell and an oil and gas cell. Discussions with ASML — and specifically with their physics director, Jan Willem Martens — led to the start of a physics cell, for which Joeri Voets was hired (Voets also stayed twelve years and eventually became the managing director of TMC West Netherlands). In 2006, Edwin de Zeeuw came on board, who later became the director of TMC Mechatronica), and Marjolein Berkers, who would become responsible for TMC Manufacturing Support (and later became the start-up director for new cells in the Netherlands). And in January 2007, Thijs Manders "lured away" one of Jan Mengelers' talents, Katja Pahnke, who was running the products and materials department of Mengelers' focus area.

Katja Pahnke is a determined, self-confident woman in her early fifties (like more and more people nowadays, she doesn't disclose her age in her CV), with a slight German accent. She received her professional training — as a biological analyst — while working at a waste processing company in the northwest of Germany. Later, she studied chemical engineering in Oldenburg. She moved to the Netherlands in 1999, to work for Philips (and do her master thesis) and later TNO. When I interviewed her in early 2019, she explained that her transition to TMC was in fact solicited by TNO's Jan Mengelers himself. "He posted me at TMC to find good engineers for TNO," she said. By hiring her, Thijs Manders more or less hijacked that initiative. Over a decade later, Jan Mengelers was still smiling about this move. "When Katja went to TMC, Thijs in fact got himself an ambassador. She knew very well what kind of people TNO needed."[7]

In Katja Pahnke's view, her transition was a win-win for both TNO and TMC. "At the time, TNO's culture was still quite bureaucratic. The institute wanted to become more flexible and market-oriented and had started working on a project basis, so the situation was extremely suitable for bringing in young, fresh people who would work on a project for two or three years." TMC, on the other hand, wanted to expand its business cells. When Katja Pahnke first got to know the company, there were five: Embedded Software, ERP (SAP) Professionals, Engineering Professionals, Mechatronics and Physics (plus the two "would-be" cells of Field Service and Manufacturing Support). Pahnke: "TNO also wanted support in chemical, automotive and mechanical; so Thijs asked me to form three news cells for those specializations as well." Jan Mengelers accepted her step graciously and even suggested that she take ten TNO engineers along with her, as a basis for the new cells. She was hesitant about that, however. "I said: I want to put them through their paces, but I will reject them if I have any doubts. They have to fit in the entrepreneurial model and spirit of TMC. None of them made it." Many people regarded her rejection of the TNO-ten as an almost offensive move, but she found that it also gave the new cells a high-quality image: "Apparently you had to be very good to be able to join." It proved no problem to find these very good people, she said. "At the end of 2007, so within a year, we had fifty people working for TNO, all excellent, entrepreneurial engineers."[8]

BUSINESS CELL MODELS
A tool for managing professionals

TMC's cell structure originates from a line of managerial and organizational thinking that gained traction in the 1990s and 2000s and centers around keywords like self-management, autonomy and independent work teams. A series of inspirational leaders had already applied these ideas in their organizations before TMC was founded. The Brazilian entrepreneur Ricardo Semler became famous with his Semco Style; in the Netherlands, Eckart Wintzen (1939–2008) built his software consultancy BSO around them; and later, in the same country, Jos de Blok set up his cell-structured organization for district nursing, called Buurtzorg.

If you want to know how TMC took the business cell model to the next level, read this text box first.

Back to TMC's introduction day, December 2019. Sven Bongartz, cell director of TMC Mechanical was hosting a group of highly educated employees who had just joined TMC. He told them how Thijs Manders started the company. "Companies like ASML need highly educated people. There is business in providing them with a flexible workforce. But how can we give them what they need? For that purpose, Manders copied Eckart Wintzen's model of business cells."

THE ECKART WINTZEN (BSO) STYLE
In 1990, the Dutch software consultancy BSO published an annual report for children. When young Esther Wittenberg interviewed CEO Eckart Wintzen about it for the Dutch daily newspaper NRC Handelsblad, he explained to her in simple terms how his company differed from others. "We split our 1500 people into thirty different small companies, which can operate in a completely independent way. Most larger companies have a fancy director, and below him there are even more directors, secretaries and personal assistants, a department for acquisition, a sales department, a project office, a division for production. Well, we don't have those. If BSO's Eindhoven office needs new people, they can publish a vacancy on their own. That's much more fun, because they can choose a nice guy they want to work with."[9]

Wintzen had founded BSO in 1976 (via a buy-out) and left it two decades later, in 1996. In 2007, a year before his death, he published *Eckart Notes*, a personal, witty and straightforward account of the dos, don'ts, whys and hows of organizing work and processes in his former company. It looked like an actual notebook you would use for jotting down quick thoughts and observations. At BSO, which was able to develop without any serious growing pains, business cells were responsible for their own operations and profit and loss. Each cell could grow to a maximum of fifty employees. When it became bigger, it would be split in two. And so on. In that way, BSO grew into a multinational company without losing its cultural DNA and its small-scale, family-like character.[10]

It wasn't Wintzen who invented the concept of self-managing teams. Experiments with such teams had, for example, been carried out in the 1950s, in the coal mines around Durham, in the northeast of England, where their introduction apparently led to a huge improvement in productivity and a decrease in sickness absence. These and other, similar experiments had been set up to offset the demotivating effects of routine work and of breaking up activities into small subtasks, which had become common and increasingly problematic in the early 20th century. After World War II, social scientists at the British Tavistock Institute for Human Relations assembled ideas about better work conditions in an overarching "sociotechnique" theory, which eventually found its way to business schools.[11]

At first the sociotechnique theory and the concept of self-management did not acquire a big following. That had changed in the 1990s when increasing international competition forced companies to offer lower prices, better quality and greater flexibility. A number of them tried to do this by installing self-managing, project-oriented teams.[12] According to the Dutch consultant Pierre van Amelsvoort, who wrote a book about self-managing teams in 2003, competitive pressures were not the only driving forces behind them. Another was the increasing number of highly trained professionals in many lines of business who would not be pushed into standardized work routines and work environments, and demanded autonomy and independence. "A relatively large gap had grown between the level of education of many people and what was actually being asked of them at work," Van Amelsvoort wrote.[13]

THE RICARDO SEMLER (SEMCO) STYLE

An example of the potential success of self-governance was Semco, which in the 1990s became one of the most beloved companies to work for in Brazil. The Semco story started with a personal crisis. A few years after Ricardo Semler had succeeded his father as CEO of the company, he collapsed due to stress. He decided to make some changes. He reduced the twelve management layers to three, stripped executives of their privileges (such as special parking places), stopped the obligation for workers to punch in and out, and abolished mandatory company clothing. After a while, he went even further. He allowed employees to set their own salary levels, introduced self-managing teams and profit sharing, let employees choose and evaluate their own bosses, gave them access to the financial data of the company and helped them set up their own business. Meanwhile, revenues grew from $30 million in 1988 to $212 million in 2003. Thanks to this success and a book Ricardo Semler wrote about his ideas in 1993, these revolutionary changes became known as Semco Style. Semler acquired a large following and became a popular business guru. After 2001, he gradually sold his shares and changed Semco Group into an investment company.[14]

THE JOS DE BLOK (BUURTZORG) STYLE

Eckart Wintzen and Ricardo Semler showed that self-management and organizational growth can go hand in hand. That this can also work in the public sector was proven by Dutchman Jos de Blok, a district nurse. In 2007, he and four friends began their own organization for district nursing and called it Buurtzorg (neighborhood care). They started from the idea that "it should not become a company but a movement that should restore the authority of the district nurse, provide personal care to vulnerable people and organize operations in a way that would benefit both patients and nurses: small-scale and therefore without managers."[15]

De Blok was not an academic type, but during his college years he became interested in sociological and organizational issues. Later, he set up Buurtzorg with the deep belief that employees don't need a manager if they are intrinsically motivated and feel the appeal of a larger ideal. Many did. Year after year, Buurtzorg attracted hundreds of district nurses who signed up because they were disappointed in regular health care and wanted to set up their own neighborhood teams. At Buurtzorg, they don't work in separate teams for washing, putting on stockings and providing medication. Buurtzorg's nursing teams schedule and manage their own work, and solve all the problems they encounter.[16]

Eight years after the start, Buurtzorg had nine thousand employees in eight hundred self-managing neighborhood teams which took care of 55,000 clients. Annual revenues amounted to €280 million.[17]

DAVID MAISTER AND MATHIEU WEGGEMAN ON MANAGING PROFESSIONALS

One of the earliest authors on managing professionals and the connection between performance and motivation is David Maister, who was a professor at Harvard Business School from 1979–1985. He put his ideas on paper in his book *Managing the Professional Service Firm* (New York, 1993), in which he argued that all professional performance arises from a strong motivation. This will lead to high productivity and quality, and to success on the market. As a result, the organization will be able to offer high salaries, real chances of promotion and interesting work, which in turn will lead to even stronger motivation. How to ignite such a spiral? It all starts with recruitment, Maister argued. When selecting professionals, one should not only look at their intellectual and technical capabilities but also at their ambition and energy. To prevent disappointment and demotivation potential, new employees should be made aware what the job requires and what it will really look like. Maister warned against glossy recruitment brochures in which workload, work variation, contacts with clients, coaching and other things that are relevant for young professionals are presented in a slick, polished way. This may at first attract many new people, "But [it] will turn against the company when the new employees are confronted with reality."[18]

Buurtzorg founder Jos de Blok got his inspiration from Mathieu Weggeman, a Dutch consultant and professor in organizational sciences. In his book *Leading Professionals. Don't!* (2008), Weggeman cited the famous Canadian management scientist Henry Mintzberg, who wrote: "Knowledge workers cannot be managed by dictating rules and procedures or by applying information systems." Weggeman fully agrees. Though the title of his book is provoking, the contents are nuanced. Weggeman does not conclude that anarchy is the only alternative. "The challenge is of course to create a workable balance between anarchy and planning and control."[19]

According to Weggeman, managers of knowledge-intensive organizations should realize that most of their employees are highly motivated. They have studied for years to be able to do what they do and generally have good self-managing capabilities. They shouldn't be bothered with bureaucratic obligations like forms, reports, rules and procedures. Instead they should be facilitated to plan and check their own working processes. Productivity and quality will follow. Why? Because real professionals would rather do something right than wrong.[20]

HOW TO ADOPT A SUCCESSFUL MODEL

After Eckert Wintzen's death in 2008, the economist and consultant Gyuri Vergouw wrote in an obituary: "What Wintzen and his charismatic approach accomplished, did not work elsewhere or hardly."[21] And yes, when Wintzen had bought Philips Electronics' internal software consultancy department, in two steps (1990 and 1996), the earlier family culture had begun to change, and after the company had been acquired by the French Atos group in 2000, its cell structure had disappeared.

Semco Style got a wider distribution, maybe because Ricardo Semler actively disseminated it. Today, his Semco Style Institute has offices in the Netherlands, United Kingdom, Germany, South Africa and India and offers training programs for consultants, interim managers, corporate change-makers and entrepreneurs. It has developed a network of certified Semco Style consultants who help organizations make the transformation to democratic management or self-management.[22]

One person who adopted the Semco Style is Dutch entrepreneur Allard Droste. He completely transformed a traditional and hierarchical Dutch metal company into a self-managing, highly motivated and profitable working environment. In his book *Semco in de polder* (Semco in the Polder) he described how he adopted several of Semler's principles, but also gave a Dutch twist to their implementation.[23]

Buurtzorg, the Dutch organisation for district nursing, also attracted a lot of attention from abroad. Today, Buurtzorg-like care concepts can be found in the United Kingdom, China, India, Taiwan, Germany and South Korea. "Implementation is not always easy," Gertje van Roessel, a Buurtzorg employee for international contacts said in a Dutch TV documentary. She mentioned a Swedish nurse who had worked at Buurtzorg in the Netherlands and wanted to bring the concept to Sweden, but "was faced with entirely different care and financing systems than in the Netherlands." In Asian countries, employees may find it hard to work in a Buurtzorg-style non-hierarchical structure. "The idea of self-management was a bridge too far in Japan," said Van Roessel, "so, for now, we work there with a head nurse who manages the teams in a coaching style."[24]

TMC'S CELL STRUCTURE: ECKART WINTZEN UPGRADED

The key to adopting successful models is adaptation, so it would seem. When Thijs Manders became inspired by Eckart Wintzen's cell structure, he understood that he should not copy every detail but had to add a touch of his own. And that's what he did.

He adopted the critical size idea. When TMC cells grow beyond around fifty, they are split. Maybe not exactly at fifty but a bit later, so the split-up cells will have enough volume to begin with. When a new regional office or new country office is set up, it starts out as if it were a new business cell with a similar structure: a director, a few account managers and a small support staff, initially not more than an office manager. Again, once such an office grows significantly beyond fifty, it will be split into expertise-based business cells. In November 2019, I interviewed Jaskaran Sandhu, one of the directors of TMC Belgium. We will meet him more extensively later in this book. The Belgian office, located in Brussels, was set up in 2014 as TMC's first international venture. By the end of 2019, it had grown to about 180 employeneurs. "Given that the cells ideally are between forty and eighty people," Sandhu said, "today we have three cells. So obviously we have more competences in one cell. We have a certain grouping of competences. In my cell, we focus on physics, nanotechnology and data technology. These are niche markets, core research activities. You don't have many consultancies in Belgium doing that. The other three cells focus on software, electronics and IT."[25]

In other respects, there are significant differences between Wintzen's cells and TMC's cells. A major one is that TMC's cells do not produce services and don't employ teams of professionals who work on common projects (although, as we will see, some experiments along that line are being considered). Their members are deployed on an individual basis, to work at companies which will often put them in project teams but are themselves not necessarily organized in cell structures.

If TMC's cells produce anything, then it is people — highly qualified people. With that goal in mind, the company has given its cells a triple purpose. Yes, like Wintzen's cells they are **business** cells, with their own profit and loss responsibility, but they are also a method to organize the company's areas of expertise, and — equally important — they are a social environment in which TMC's employeneurs can meet like-minded professionals.[26]

Eckart Wintzen was well aware of the social aspect of business cells, but TMC took that aspect a step further by actively using the cells to support and stimulate its employees in their professional and personal development. In that sense, they may be regarded as Wintzen-plus or Wintzen-upgraded.

As **business** cells, with a profit and loss responsibility, TMC's cells are, to a large degree, self-managed. Because their main product is the "employeneur," with all kinds of qualities and expertise, they don't need much support staff. Decentralized decision-making allows country and business cell managers to fully focus on attracting new talent and new clients.[27]

In France, for example, TMC has four regional offices: in Paris, Nantes, Toulouse and Sophia Antipolis (near Nice). When I interviewed Loïc le Mené, CEO of TMC Paris, in November 2019, he told me, "With TMC, you are your own boss, the structure of management is really lean. I have direct access to Emmanuel Mottrie [CEO of the TMC group] and for the financial aspect to Rogier and his team [Rogier van Beek, CFO of the TMC group]. We have one board meeting every month, and then we have informal calls, and I have contact with my fellow CEOs in other countries. Twice a year we have a CEO meeting and keep in touch by Skype and telephone. And in France it is more like weekly calls with the other directors, but it is not regular."

People at the core

Autonomous teams should be based on a vision, Pierre van Amelsvoort wrote: "A vision that shows people are the most important capital in the organization and that a self-managing team is a powerful tool to cherish and use that capital." TMC did just that. People are its core business, supporting the professional and personal development of its employeneurs is seen as critical to the company's success. This resonates with Ricardo Semler's vision, who is often quoted to have said, "The purpose of work is not to make money. The purpose of work is to make the employees, whether working stiffs or top executives, feel good about life."[28]

GOING TOO FAST?

When Katja Pahnke joined TMC in May 2007, the company was moving ahead at top speed. Just half a year before, in November 2006, TMC had offered a quarter of its shares to the public, via Alternext. This young stock exchange for medium-sized enterprises was part of Euronext. It had been active in Paris since 2005 and in Brussels and Amsterdam since September 2006 — so just two months before the TMC offering. Why this move? When I asked him over a decade later, Thijs Manders said, "It was a way to get more media attention, of course, and for me personally, it was also because I was looking for a challenge, for more complexity in my entrepreneurship." The IPO gave him the means to acquire Adapté, a civil engineering consultancy based in the city of Utrecht, in the heart of the Netherlands. The acquisition price was €17.6 million plus a maximum variable amount of €2.8 million, dependent on TMC's 2007 profit. It was paid in cash (75 percent) and convertible stock (25 percent). Since TMC's IPO had brought in €10 million, the company issued another €10 million in convertible bonds to pay for the acquisition. It was a big chunk to swallow, an acquisition, to be sure, but it could also have been presented as a merger. When the sale was formalized, in July 2007, TMC had 235 employees, Adapté 170. The year before, TMC had generated income of €14.1 million, Adapté around €10 million. Each had made a profit of €2.8 million. The press release described the acquisition as an "excellent supplement" to TMC's services, an "expansion of [its] technical competences" and as offering "opportunities in new markets."[29]

It wasn't to be a happy marriage. Adapté's former owners — the brothers Henk and Wim Bredewoud — had agreed to help integrate their company into TMC. However, soon after the sale, Wim became overstressed and had to withdraw. Meanwhile, Henk proved hesitant to introduce the employeneurship model in his former shop (which he still managed). Thijs Manders remembered, "He said: only ten percent of my people are employeneurs, the others are not. I said: no, everyone is an employeneur but to a different degree. You have to develop it in them."[30]

As TMC continued to grow and flourish, the newly acquired branch didn't. In the meantime, the international economic situation worsened. Just a month after the formalization of the Adapté acquisition, international stock prices began to fall, and during the rest of the summer of 2007 more and more financial institutions — first in the USA but soon also in Europe — began to report losses and depreciations, mainly on their so-called mortgage-backed securities. What began as a mortgage crisis soon evolved into a widespread banking crisis, which continued to deepen and eventually — in 2008 — led to the downfall of numerous banks, including major ones like Bear Stearns in the USA and Fortis in the Benelux countries (the former was bought by JP Morgan, with a huge loan from the federal government; the latter was bought by the Dutch state). It was only a matter of time before the "real" economy would be affected as well. On January 21, 2008, TMC once again moved its offices, this time to the Flight Forum, a business park at Eindhoven Airport. Within months after the move, an alarming number of manufacturing companies in the USA and Europe began to issue turnover and profit warnings. Among them was ASML, one of TMC's major clients: its turnover was expected to be ten percent lower than in the previous year. In July, this expectation was lowered further, to minus twenty percent. The reality turned out even worse. At the end of the year, ASML's turnover had shrunk almost a quarter, from €3.8 billion to €2.9 billion. And the worst was yet to come: in 2009, ASML's sales plummeted to just €1.6 billion, an unbelievable sixty percent below the 2007 level.[31]

Inevitably, Thijs Manders received an invitation to a difficult meeting with ASML's top management. "You have 150 people here, they told me. That will be difficult to maintain." The number would have to go down considerably, and on top of that ASML required — as in 2002 — that TMC reduce its fees by fifteen percent. Yet, other agencies were hurt harder. Manders: "Most of their secondments at ASML were phased out, but we kept seventy-five people."[32]

Unlike the 2002 crisis, TMC did not survive the 2009 crisis un-scathed. Revenues went down from €42 million to €37 million; the number of employeneurs from 460 to 387 (at year-end); operational income (EBITDA) from €6.1 million to €2.7 million. A severe crisis in the building industry hit civil engineering firm Adapté so hard that it just barely stayed above break-even point. Since projections for the building sector were bleak, the TMC board of management and the supervisory board decided to arrange an impairment test. This made clear that Adapté's book value had to be depreciated by €6.2 million, resulting in a net loss of €4.7 million. Fortunately, TMC's balance sheet was strong — after the depreciation it still had around €15 million in equity and a debt/equity ratio of 37/63. On top of a depre-ciation, Adapté also needed downsizing, stronger management and a more active integration into the TMC group and the employeneurs model. In the first half of 2009, the number of Adapté professionals went down fifteen percent, as with the rest of the group, its manage-ment team was reinforced and Henk Bredewoud retreated to the role of strategic advisor. In the next two years, Adapté was transformed into a TMC business cell for civil engineering, and, in 2011, the group stopped using Adapté as a brand name altogether.[33]

Had TMC overeaten itself with such a major acquisition? Had it expanded too fast? One might say so. The group definitely needed a sharper focus. At the outset of the 2009 crisis, it consisted of three branches, or member companies as TMC called them. Of these, Adapté was already discussed in the paragraph above. The second was TMC Assessment & Development, a limited liability company, majority-owned by TMC and still managed by Freek van Bedaf. Its coaching services were of course vital to the employeneurship model. Still, it might be regarded as a supplier rather than one of the company's core business cells. It was therefore decided that it would best be continued as a separate identity and was (in 2010) transformed into the Pontes Group.[34]

The biggest member company, and most in need of restructuring, was TMC Technology & ICT, which included the initial TMC Embedded Software branch, TMC SAP Professionals and all the newly formed business cells. To begin with, it was split up, with the clear intention to expand and strengthen the technology part and gradually phase out the ICT part. Most of its business cells and 260 of its around 300 employeneurs became part of the new TMC Technology member company. The embedded software cell, which one could have imagined as part of the ICT branch, was instead allotted to TMC Technology as well. Within the new TMC ICT member company, a couple of small loss-making activities were discontinued; as a result, only the SAP professionals cell (with thirty-seven professionals) remained.[35]

Following this, it also made sense to restructure the board of management. In the preceding years, the number of cells had increased and their directors were all senior people. TMC Technology had its own management team, consisting of the cell directors and member company director Ronald van Gerwen, who had made his career at ASML, an ICT consultancy and Assembléon (a former Philips Electronic Manufacturing Technology subsidiary and producer of "pick and place" machines which had been divested to a private equity company). The Adapté Construction & Civil Engineering "member company" had its own management team as well, while TMC ICT consisted of only one cell. It seemed a bit top-heavy to maintain a four-man board above this well-staffed layer of middle managers.

Moreover, the atmosphere in the management board — comprised of Thijs Manders, CFO Rogier van Beek, and Luuk Jeuken and Roy Roosen (chief commercial officer and chief operational officer, respectively) — was rather tense. After the supervisory board had sought independent external advice, the decision was made to flatten the top structure. As Thijs Manders put it during one of my interviews with him, "We went back to the cells." The board of management was first reduced to a two-person body, consisting of Manders and (then) 35-year-old Rogier van Beek, who had been working in controlling functions at NXP and ST-Ericsson and had been appointed as TMC's chief financial officer in January 2009. Roosen and Jeuken left; the company bought back their shares. In 2010, Luud Engels, a then 51-year old electronics engineer and an experienced project manager came over from Assembléon to become the new chief operational officer.[36]

THE BUY-OUT

Because TMC was publicly listed, the departure of Roosen and Jeuken had to be published. This caused some adverse publicity, but that soon subsided when TMC quickly found back its path to growth. As Thijs Manders put it, "We grew with 'our fingers in our noses.'" (originally a French expression popular among racing cyclists, meaning "effortlessly"). By the end of 2010, revenues, earnings and the number of employeneurs (433) were almost back at the 2008 year-end level. In investors' lingo, this could be labeled "a strong recovery," and when TMC presented its 2010 figures, it proudly announced an extra anniversary dividend. In 2011 growth accelerated further. The number of employeneurs climbed to 478 and revenues shot up from €42 million to €52 million, resulting in earnings before tax of €8 million. Manders: "It was a top year!"[37]

It was such a top year that TMC was courted, and certainly not by the least of its competitors but by the big French engineering consultancy/secondment firm Altran, which offered to buy all of TMC's shares. At the time, Altran was about thirty times as big as TMC in revenues and even more in staff. However, the French group was also debt-ridden and in heavy weather. It was involved in a restructuring and depreciation exercise like the one TMC had gone through two years earlier and had to report considerable EBITDA losses in both 2010 and 2011. In return for acquiring TMC, Altran offered the owners twenty percent of its share capital, then worth about €57 million. That may sound like a nice sum, but in view of the French group's financial uncertainties Thijs Manders and his co-shareholder Jan van Rijt weren't particularly pleased with the form of payment: in shares. Manders also didn't like the fact that Altran was just going through another change of CEOs, and — last but not least — he doubted that the TMC's employeneur model would survive such a takeover. The takeover didn't materialize (Manders and Van Rijt may have felt some regret when Altran was sold to Cap Gemini in 2019 for €3.6 billion. With twenty percent of the shares they would have been very rich indeed).[38]

By that time, Manders decided that he would end the company's public listing. Although the Alternext exchange was reasonably popular in France, it had never become a success in the Netherlands. After five years, only two Dutch stocks and two Dutch bonds were listed on it, there wasn't much trading going on and plans began to circulate to close the Dutch Alternext market altogether. Manders didn't want to move the stock to the regular Amsterdam AEX exchange. "By that time I knew I wanted to expand TMC abroad, and if you are publicly listed you have to report every single fart."[39]

Somewhere in 2012, the TMC board was meeting in the company's offices in Utrecht, which were the home base of the TMC Construction member company (formerly Adapté). That year, the company had merged its management and supervisory boards into a one-tier board on which Thijs Manders served as CEO and (executive) chairman. In the same building were also the offices of Gilde Buy Out Partners, a Dutch investment fund. Paul Schouwenaar, one of TMC's non-executive directors, had done business with Gilde, and during a break he paid them a short visit. Within weeks, TMC and Gilde had entered into serious talks about a buy-out that would allow the company to delist itself. Just before Christmas 2012, a final deal was reached. The stock price was set at €18.75, which valued the company at about €70 million. Gilde invested about half of this and acquired a 51 percent majority stake. The rest of the deal was financed with loans from ING and Rabobank. This construction, which the company could easily afford since it had hardly any debt, allowed both Manders and Van Rijt to re-invest part of their proceeds and remain major (but minority) shareholders *and* pocket around €7 million and €8 million, respectively.[40]

Now TMC was ready for its next step: across the border.

CHAPTER 3

TRANSPARENCY, THAT'S THE DISRUPTIVE THING

MEET TWO OF TMC'S 'OLD GUYS'

First Bert Stohr (56) ....

Bert Stohr has the body of a racing cyclist (which is one of his hobbies) and the mind of a high-speed motorcycle. His head is shaven, his figure slim. He speaks fast. If there exists a technical genome, Bert has it. As a child he was always working on bicycles, go-karts and model trains. At university he studied precision mechanics and now, 56 years old, he still loves to make things (another of his hobbies is home improvement). When we interviewed him in September 2019, he was working at Sioux System Assembly, a manufacturer of high-tech modules, systems and machines in the Eindhoven region. Sioux is located in a non-descript building in one of Eindhoven's industrial areas. Part of the manufacturing hall is freely accessible, another part is fitted up as a clean room, in which people work in a soft, yellowish light. The offices above the hall are very basically decorated, but they feel agreeable: this is a place of concentration, devoid of distractions. Bert was in one of the offices.[1]

His handshake is firm, his eyes are bright. And, since he's working on a variety of products simultaneously for a variety of clients, he's extremely busy. "Of course the clients all want to be served on request, and they all demand the same amount of attention," he said. "I've never been so busy." But, he added, "All my projects are equally exciting."

Stohr is an inventor and an entrepreneur. Right after technical university, a medical start-up offered to develop a product he had conceived while still studying: a catheter with a built-in transmitter-receiver that would be able to project and transmit a cross-section image of the inside of blood vessels. "It could be used to check arteries for plaque and inspect the results of balloon angioplasty and/or the placing of stents," Bert explained. He stayed with the company — DuMed — for six years, from 1990–1996. Then it was bought by an American firm. "I went to the USA to work for them, but after half a year it was clear to me that I wasn't going to make my career there."

Why not? Maybe because the buyer wasn't interested in developing the product further but only in selling it. That's not where Bert Stohr's fascination lies. He went back to the Netherlands to work for ASM International, a manufacturer of wafer processing machines for the semiconductor industry (ASM is not to be confused with ASML, but it is historically related to this company, which in fact started as a joint venture of ASM and Philips Electronics). There he found his natural habitat. "When R&D engineers come up with a new invention, it has to be translated into a producible product. That doesn't always go smoothly. At ASM we formed an 'in-between' team of engineers who could act as translators between the inventors and the production people who could pick up a prototype and make it suitable for serial production."

Stohr stayed at ASM for eleven years. But in 2007, he got tired. Not of working at ASM but of the 130km commute — twice daily — between his home in the Eindhoven region and his workplace in Almere, a town near Amsterdam. As a manager of one of ASM's engineering departments he regularly hired temporary staff from various high-tech and R&D consultancies, including TMC. So he decided to ask one of TMC's account managers to find him a job closer to home. Initially, he expected this to be a transitional phase: he would do a couple of projects for one or two of TMC's clients and then move to another steady job. But once he was on board, "I discovered that TMC had an enormous added value for me: because of the flexibility it offers me, the chance to take a look behind the scenes of various companies, the ability to use my experience to help those companies on their way forward, the opportunity to broaden my own expertise and knowledge — all of those things."

Various companies, in his case, means seven. During his twelve years at TMC, Stohr was sent to Océ van der Grinten (a manufacturer of copiers, for which he developed the packaging of a new machine), IAI Industrial Systems (where he worked on the concept of a new welding machine for solar panels) and ABB (where he helped to start up a production line for electric vehicle chargers). Then he helped Fonckel — a young and innovative lighting manufacturer in Eindhoven — to start up production, designed and implemented a new multi-client production process for Wilting Components (also in Eindhoven), and helped the construction company Heijmans to improve its product development processes. Since April 2018, he's been at Sioux Systems, where he's working on a wafer stepper, a photolithographic machine with a so-called step-and-repeat camera to produce miniaturized patterns on coated disks, which are then used to build integrated circuits (chips). This particular machine — described by Stohr as a "robust" one of 2.5 × 2.5 × 2 meters — is to be used in the production of powerful multicore processors.

As a TMC employeneur, Stohr began as an "industrializator" and systems architect and gradually grew towards more senior positions. At Sioux Systems he is a "new product introduction project leader." That development towards leading roles just happened, it wasn't the result of his ambition, he says. "The companies I work for need my expertise to solve a problem with a product or with production. But soon after my arrival they tend to ask me to take the lead in the project, maybe because they see that this role comes naturally to me."

When we ask Bert whether his relationship with TMC has (had) any downsides, he can't think of any. Really? No imperfections at all? Sorry, no. So even if some readers may think that this sounds too good to be true, I'll put it in print. And why is the match so perfect? Bert doesn't hesitate. "By regularly moving to a new client, I keep learning, and that's important to me. Plus, I love to share my expertise with my clients and to be appreciated for that."

... then Bernardus Venema (59)

In 2010 Dräger, the German manufacturer of medical equipment, closed its ventilator production unit in Best, near Eindhoven. Bernardus Venema, an electronics engineer, then 49 years old, had been working there for seven years. As a "life cycle engineer," he had been responsible for the continuous improvement of a specific module of one of Dräger's systems. Then he lost that job. Someone gave him a tip: talk to TMC. He had never heard of the group, but took the advice anyway.[2]

When we interviewed him, in September 2019, Bernardus was working at his sixth TMC client. His first project was at the Dutch branch of Ushio Xtreme Technologies, a Japanese industrial lighting company, where he developed training material for service engineers. He stayed three years. Then he went to VDL Group, a Dutch manufacturer of buses, assembler of passenger cars and subcontractor for ASML, to help prepare the production line for a new product. He spent half a year at candle maker Bolsius, where he tracked down production bottlenecks and helped solve them. In 2014–2015, he worked for a year as an instructor at Rockpanel, a manufacturer of exterior cladding panels, and assisted this company with the improvement of its production processes. Client number five was Philips Handheld Diagnostics, a subsidiary that was developing portable blood testers. Here he had a role similar to that of his colleague Bert Stohr: to act as an intermediary between developers and production people. He left in May 2017, a few months before Philips announced the discontinuation of the subsidiary due to a lack of commercial prospects for the product.[3]

Anteryon — Venema's latest client — isn't hard to find. It's one of three companies (at the time of the interview) in Brainport Industries Campus Eindhoven, a large, brand new collective building located in a small forest near Eindhoven Airport. Anteryon was spun off from Philips in 2006. It makes optical precision components like laser modules, optical test and measurement modules, and special lenses. In 2019, it was bought by the Chinese company Jingfang Optoelectronics, which is based in Suzhou, close to Shanghai.[4]

Bernardus went to work at Anteryon in 2017, the company moved there in August 2018. His hair is crew cut, he wears glasses, sturdy hiking shoes and a blue polo shirt with the TMC logo; his accent reveals that he grew up in the southern province of Limburg, where his parents migrated to from Groningen, in the north of the Netherlands. He works in one of the cubicles along the wall of a long, corridor-like, rather dark and disorderly room. On the other side are doors to production rooms, which are partly openly accessible, partly cleanrooms where everybody wears special, light-blue clothing, gloves and shoe covers. Bernardus' cubicle — just big enough for a chair and a desk with two computer screens — is surrounded by panels on which he has stuck some papers. He shows one of them, a crossword puzzle he developed to test operators who work with Anteryon's products. Question 13: how do you clean a specific type of lens (five letters)? Answer: water (distilled, that is, but that wouldn't fit in the puzzle). He can't show any other questions, since they would reveal company secrets, he says.

So what is he doing here? "When I came here, the company had just developed a machine module that would go into series production," he explained. "However, the developer was the only person who could put it together. My job was to write a set of instructions for the operators on the future assembly line. I sat down beside the developer, asked him to build the module and took notes and photos of every single step. After he had corrected my notes, I built one myself, with him watching me. This way we developed — step by step — a set of instructions the production operators could work with." It took about two months to come up with this first set. "Then we fine-tuned and improved them and developed specific tools to speed up the assembly procedure." This perfecting phase took another six months.

Venema makes a simple drawing of a laser beam to show what the module is about. A laser cutter cuts through a material in three directions:

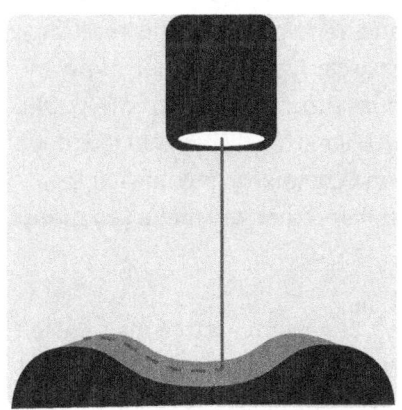

from left to right, from top to bottom, and vertically, through the material. During the cutting process, the distance between the laser and the material will vary in all three directions, so it is necessary to constantly adapt its focus. "Since lenses are relatively heavy, they limit the speed of the cutter's movements." This module contains several tiny mirrors and the electronics to tilt them synchronously with the laser. "This way, the laser can be kept in perfect focus and do the cutting thirty times faster."

Explaining complicated things is one of Bernardus' strengths. "I can talk with a professor and explain to my grandmother what he told me," he says. It's the teacher in him. He proudly recounts an instruction method he developed at Rockpanel. He fitted each of their production machines with a QR code. The operators were given a tablet. When scanning the code with the tablet, they would be shown a short video of how to operate the machine. Scanning a second, red QR code would alert the maintenance department in case of a machine failure.

When he lost his job at Dräger in 2010 and went to talk with TMC, Bernardus was reluctant. "I didn't really want to work in consultancy, I wanted a steady job." But when he met with the TMC account manager, he was immediately won over. The first gesture that caused that shift was that he was offered both a fixed contract and the same salary as at Dräger's. "TMC did not exploit the fact that I was losing my job there." The second gesture was even better. "I wanted more than TMC's regular twenty-five annual leave days. I was 49 years old at the time and had lost jobs several times, so I had decided to start a part-time education to become a physics teacher. Being qualified as a teacher would be a back-up, in case that happened again. The TMC account manager said: how about five extra leave days and us paying the tuition?

While TMC financed his teacher training at university level, Bernardus invested his evening hours and his leave during his teaching internship. "They even gave me a lease car for the duration of my internship, which I did in a town that was difficult to reach with public transport." Why would TMC go to such lengths? "They told me: it will broaden your knowledge of physics and chemistry and mechanics, and help you develop your didactic skills — that will make you more valuable to us."

His enthusiasm for TMC hasn't faded. "I never regretted my decision, not a single day." On the contrary, over the years it has increased and now concerns the entire TMC package: "The quarterly cell meetings, the pizza sessions, the coaches, the personal budget for extra training or courses, the freedom — if I don't like it here anymore I can call my account manager and ask him to find me another job. And he will do that, and find someone to take my place. That really gives me a sense of being in control." At all of his projects, his clients have asked him to come work for them on a regular basis. "I told all of them: sorry, I'm staying with TMC."

▌ THE DNA WORKSHOP

High noon at Eindhoven's High Tech Campus. It's November 12, 2019. Across the vast grounds, groups of people are stretching their legs and having a bit of fresh air while eating a sandwich. TMC's lunchroom is filled with the animated chatter of sixteen account managers and cell directors from all parts of the group: Spain, France, Sweden, Belgium, the Netherlands, the United States even. They are here for TMC Fundamentals, an intensive three-day program. Prenella Patterson from New York can't get over the view. She points outside to a flock of sheep grazing peacefully on a fenced-off plot of grass. "I come from a big city. I know what cows and horses are. But sheep! There are so many of them!"[5]

The sixteen participants have been appointed to their present positions somewhere in the last six months. Now it's time to marinate them in the company's culture. Training programs like these are held twice a year. They are loaded with lectures, workshops and networking opportunities. Today is reserved for a DNA workshop, subtitled: in-depth knowledge of our business model & how to use it efficiently. Before it starts, the participants have to make some important choices, though. They concern tonight's dinner menu. Will they have salmon or steak tartare, a lobster bisque or a mushroom soup, veal cheeks or sea bass, dame blanche or cheese? Half of them go for the meat, the other half for fish.

The meeting room has one glass wall, which offers a broad view of the campus grounds. The opposite wall brings a different inspiration, a quote: "Simplicity is the ultimate sophistication," attributed to Leonardo, yes, *the* Leonardo. The wall describes him as an architect, inventor, engineer, philosopher, physicist, chemist, anatomist, sculptor and writer. How about that for a role model?

The session is moderated by Noortje van Boxtel, cell director of Manufacturing Support South (there are similar business cells in the east and west of the Netherlands). She's all enthusiasm about TMC and even calls it "too good to be true." Why? "It's a people's business. We don't make machines, we invest in human beings, to help them grow." After this galvanizing declaration, she introduces TMC's core principles, which are all about — the projector now projects a huge hand on the screen, index finger pointing at the audience — YOU.

After some discussion in sub-groups, the plenary session continues and Noortje guides the conversation along the five principles while provoking the participants' thoughts about their pros and cons. Unsurprisingly, the pros abound. The *business cells* stimulate shared responsibility and mutual commitment among the employeneurs, the group feels. They should also be a useful marketing tool: they show clients that for these fields of expertise, TMC can offer continuity and — if the client so desires — additional experts, from the same or other cells.

The YOUniversity and Entrepreneurial Lab facilities, too, are interpreted as beneficial for commercial purposes: these institutions ensure the clients that the people they get from TMC are technologically in the frontline and professionally up to date. Moreover, they are an indication of the company's preparedness to invest in its employees and to offer them opportunities — which should be good for its recruitment. There may be a con too, the group suggests: if you invest a lot in your people you'll also lose a lot if they leave. However, moderator Noortje van Boxtel downplays that risk and prefers to highlight the YOUniversity's and Lab's appeal to potential (and current) employeneurs. "These facilities allow you to plot your own career but also to get the support you need along the way." As a light-hearted underscore she gives the example of an employeneur who felt stuck in his career. "We offered him boxing training. That's always helpful."

Most participants reserved their highest praise for TMC's individual profit sharing and the long-term relationship principles. In the USA,

Prenella Patterson from New York says a consultancy offering a long-term contract would seem almost unthinkable: "In America, you're expendable".

A DEEPER LOOK INSIDE THE MODEL

Next, the five pillars of the Employeneurship model are explained in more detail.

Pillar 1: the business cell

Katja Pahnke missed TMC's 2009 crisis. After setting up three fledgling cells in 2007 (chemical, mechanical and automotive), she left TMC at the end of that year. TNO Companies, the private section of the Netherlands Organization for Applied Scientific Research, had asked her to set up and run an automotive research company in Germany, in co-operation with a German certification institute, TÜV Rheinland. The main goal of this new Dutch/German venture would be to develop and market vehicle crash tests for cars and trucks. In Germany, crisis hit her anyway. During the economic

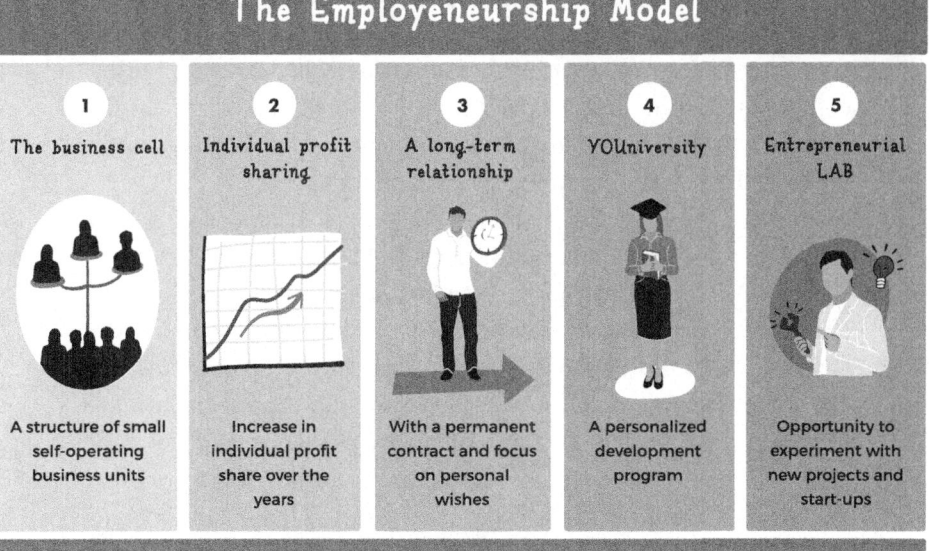

The Employeneurship Model

1	2	3	4	5
The business cell	Individual profit sharing	A long-term relationship	YOUniversity	Entrepreneurial LAB
A structure of small self-operating business units	Increase in individual profit share over the years	With a permanent contract and focus on personal wishes	A personalized development program	Opportunity to experiment with new projects and start-ups

recession following the 2007–2008 financial crisis, the automotive industry suffered badly. Pahnke: "Our revenues per impact test plummeted from twenty to ten thousand euros. That was a difficult time. We managed to reduce our losses to zero but didn't grow." [6]

In 2012, TNO Companies decided to combine forces with TASS International (now owned by Siemens) and Katja Pahnke returned to TMC. "I still had very warm connections with them," she said. "And Thijs always said: if you ever start making new plans, come talk to me." She did. In the five years of her absence, TMC had become considerably larger. "They had set up business cells in the entire product life cycle, from research to product introduction." (At the time, "product introduction" was a competence group, a group of employeneurs with similar expertise, within the manufacturing support cell). In her re-entry talks with Thijs Manders the idea of taking this expansion one step further came up. In TMC's twelve years of existence, a number of employeneurs had grown into senior roles, to which they brought not just their technical expertise but also leadership skills and (project) leadership experience. Maybe some of these seniors could work for clients as "technology executives," i.e. as managers of R&D departments or even as interim chief technology officers.

Pahnke: "I saw three goals for setting up such a technology executives cell. First, to assemble a group of people who could communicate with clients at the executive level; second, to bring TMC to the next level and stay ahead of the competition, which was beginning to copy us; and third, to jack up our image. That was sliding to the point that we would be regarded as just another a supplier of 'hired hands.' We needed to revive our image as a supplier of quality."[7]

There was a fourth goal too. Like other high-tech and R&D consultancies, TMC constantly faces "conversion pressure": the inclination of employeneurs to switch to the client's payroll. That pressure works both ways. In weak economic times some employeneurs may think that moving to a client will give them more job security and access to leadership roles. In times of economic growth and personnel shortages, on the other hand, clients may be tempted to lure consultants across their threshold and get them to stay there. Conversion pressure indicators like "churn rate" (personnel turnover rate) and

TMC's business cells: continuity, innovation & expansion

Situation at the end of 2007
10 cells

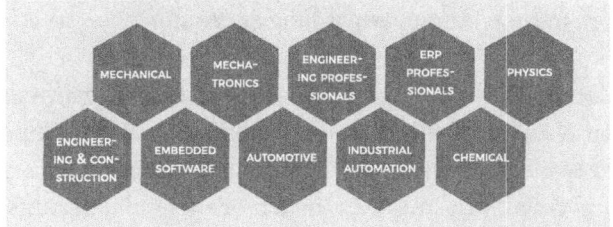

Situation at the end of 2011
14 cells

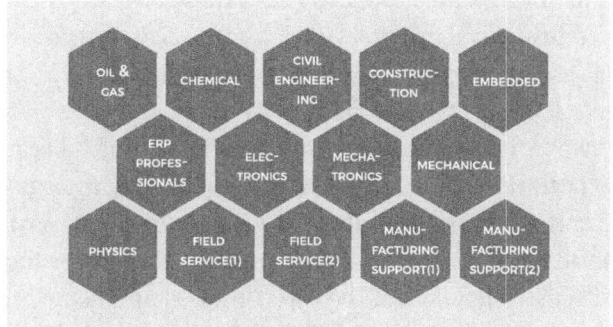

Situation at the end of 2017
18 cells

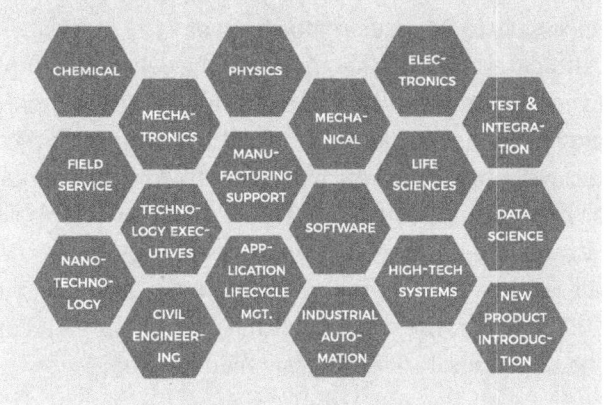

Situation at the end of 2023
NEW BUSINESS CELL OPPORTUNITIES

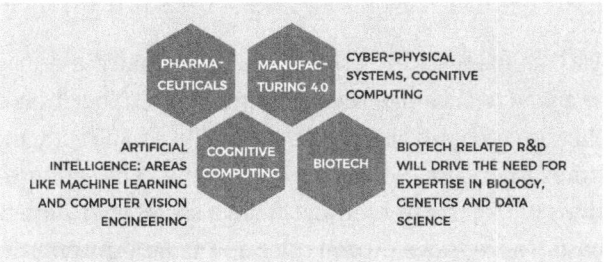

"retention rate" (the opposite) are crucial in the consultancy business, and companies in this business are always thinking of ways to retain their employees as long as possible.

Even with a model that offers its employees security, profit sharing, professional challenges and opportunities for their personal and professional development, TMC is not immune to conversion pressure and constantly analyzes the factors behind it. Around 2012, some TMC employeneurs were accepting positions at client companies because of the career opportunities these offered. The new technology executives cell might — if it was a success — offer similar opportunities and keep them on board.

It was an ambitious idea, but after some time it became clear that the expectations for candidates looking for a technology executive position had to be toned down or — to formulate it positively — needed adaptation. Pahnke said, "I set out to meet the top-ten percent of senior members of the company. Despite their seniority most of them still were too much of a technical specialist to be suited for an executive role. To help employeneurs grow towards such a role, it is necessary to introduce some form of early assessment to find future candidates and then set up a bespoke development plan for them." Even then, the demand for externally hired technology executives may never be very substantial. "The people with the required qualities will probably immediately be hired by the clients." Which could be regarded as positive for TMC because in those positions "they can be ambassadors for TMC and act as the company's eyes and ears in the market." For that reason mainly, the technology executives cell still exists (at the time of writing), even though it contributes less than 1 percent to TMC's total revenue (2017).

Building blocks for a corporate community

TMC's business cell structure — as Pahnke did — could be described as a way to organize the company into product/market combinations that are recognizable to the client. But as I already mentioned several times, there are more ways to look at it. The cells are also congregations of experts in a similar field, a social environment and a home base. These sociocultural roles don't come automatically. They have to be actively cultivated. In the twenty years of its existence, TMC has developed a wide range of tools for that.

Let's return to Bert Stohr, the bicycle-loving "old boy" from a few pages ago. Over his twelve years as an employeneur he didn't just grow in his profession and in his leadership role, he also became active in the TMC community. His cell, new product introduction (NPI) has members with diverse educational backgrounds on the one hand and on the other hand common experiences of helping companies bring new products to the production stage. "At some point we had a discussion in our cell about how to use our professional networks more actively. In the wake of that discussion I began setting up 'competence groups,' sub-groups of members with similar educational backgrounds within the cell. It took a couple of years to develop these sub-groups, but now they are a standard element in the NPI cell. We organize about four to six competence meetings per year, they are part of our 'living room feeling.'"

TMC's business cell structure

Business Managers

Cell Director

Office Managers

Around 50-70 employeneurs per business cell

Stohr also became a mentor. The company stimulates its seniors to take up such a role and thus help it in its efforts to support its new employeneurs in their professional and personal development. During his meetings with these newbies he will advise them, for example, about how to find their way in a new company — an experience he has of course repeatedly had and describes as exciting, but which, after several times, is also "somewhat fatiguing." "I tell them that, in order to be effective as a project leader, you have to know who are really in charge in the company. In many companies, there are influencers and if you manage to win them over to your ideas, the chief executive will automatically accept those ideas too."

Cell activities may take any form. For example, Casper van Dijke, a 40-year-old mechanical engineer who became a TMC member in 2012, once organized a visit by his cell colleagues (TMC Mechanical) to the company he was working at, "to show them what I was doing, in a broader sense, not just technical but also the development you experience as a technician." Van Dijke looks like a younger version of Bert Stohr: not a single gram of fat on his body, tight-fitting shirt and ditto jeans, shaven head, speaking with the speed of a machine gun. When we interviewed him, he was doing a project (for the second time) at Demcon, a producer of medical equipment in the small town of Best, near Eindhoven. We'll meet him in more detail later, but one thing is worth mentioning at this stage. It became clear during the interview that Van Dijke is a prime example of the "ambassador effect" Katja Pahnke was talking about just a few paragraphs above. He had become a TMC member in early 2012 but didn't have a project yet when mechanical cell director Toon Hermans advised him to talk to Demcon, which was a start-up at the time with a staff of just six people. In that meeting, Hermans told Van Dijke that he was going to work for Demcon himself. As a result, TMC lost a cell director to Demcon but gained an employeneur at the same firm. Van Dijke went to work at Demcon (his first stint there). Two years later, he was offered a direct contract. Interestingly, he decided to stay with TMC. Why? In part for the money: his profit share at TMC gave him a considerably higher income than Demcon offered. But the rest of the TMC package was also important: "The coaching, The Entrepreneurial Lab, the pizza sessions where you can learn from each other, the Q meetings and other events. All these things make it nice to work for TMC and create a relationship with the company."[8]

Q meeting in a brewery

Let's go to another meeting, this one of TMC's chemical (engineering) business cell. On Tuesday October 8, 2019 between 5:00 and 5:30 pm some thirty-five of its forty members trickle into the 100 Watt Café, which is part of Eindhoven's Stadsbrouwerij, a local brewery and restaurant located in a renovated former textile mill, right in the city center. They are coming for a (quarterly) Q meeting. Most are men, some women. Before the meeting starts, the members who haven't met before introduce themselves to each other. One former member has shown up, Jessica. She has left TMC to become a tech journalist and is here to say goodbye. First, there's some dinner, then a series of presentations and plenary discussions — all in English, although the majority of the attendees are Dutch.[9]

The official part of the meeting begins with announcements about new appointments and arrivals. Marjolein Berkers presents herself (she'll be acting as an interim cell director for some time) and so does Matty Bosch, who has been appointed new business manager in the city of Utrecht, where TMC wants to attract new clients. Both Marjolein and Matty project a *This is me!* sheet with photos and logos, and tell the audience about their professional education, their career, their hobbies and their friends and families.

Then it's time to talk about results. The cell has four targets, with sub-targets (every cell develops its own targets).

Target 1 is a cultural/social one: "TMC Chemical is the coolest company in the Netherlands" — a strictly qualitative target that seems to require the organization of cool events. After three quarters the cell has reached eighty percent of its desired coolness. To achieve the full hundred percent some more events have to be set up; the cell leadership is thinking of sports or a quiz evening.

Target 2 covers the members' professional and personal development: "TMC Chemical is a YOUrney of many challenging projects and development opportunities." The score, fifty-nine percent, is not impressive, due to three causes: the rather disappointing numbers of quality training courses the members have followed (these are "training courses that contribute to the individual goals and needs of employeneurs"); the also rather low number of new projects; and the low activity level of the cell's competence groups.

Target 3 is the most quantitative/financial of the four: "TMC Chemical operates brilliantly and will be rewarded for this." The cell has reached ninety percent of this target, thanks to more placements, higher revenues, a higher retention level (fewer people have left) and a higher inflow of new "high potentials".

Finally, target 4 covers the members' entrepreneurial spirit: "TMC Chemical loves employeneurship." To score well, the cell has to organize at least five pizza sessions and at least one fifth of its members should participate in an Entrepreneurial Lab project. In these respects, the cell is well on track and has reached eighty percent, bringing the total score for all four targets to 77.5 percent; so, with three more months to go, the end goal of one hundred percent is still feasible.

For employees and managers of other companies, such a mix of hard quantitative and "soft" qualitative targets may sound outlandish. At TMC, they are an integral part of the business model. TMC Chemical's Q3 Meeting ends with a discussion of a self-test the cell is organizing. At the heart is the 5Q model, which was developed by Freek van Bedaf. In the TMC culture, the letter Q has acquired a special meaning. It refers of course to the word quarter (as in a three month period) but also to the Q in IQ, EQ and three other Qs, which I shall describe in the next chapter. Originally, Q referred to the word quotient, as in intelligence quotient. Since the rise of the concept of multiple intelligences and multiple Qs — again something I will get into in the next chapter — it has also become a symbol for "quality". TMC Chemical's self-test is, in effect, an effort to determine the strengths and weaknesses of the cell's overall culture, based on a measurement of the characteristics Freek van Bedaf defined in his 5Q model. The idea is that this will help the cell's leadership to select a set of training courses that are best suited to support the members in their personal development, to help them address their Q weaknesses and to stimulate them to build on their own personal Q strengths.

The input for TMC Chemical's self-test consists of the results of the individual tests that the cell members took when they started at the company and which they have been asked to share anonymously. Collectively, these results show that new Chemical cell members generally score high on IQ (hard skills) and EQ (emotional intelligence). However, a deeper look inside the building blocks of the various Qs also reveals weaknesses such as low levels of pro-activity, of self-interest (being oriented to gaining successes and taking the credit for them) and of the strength to learn lessons from and build on successes (their own and others').

A self-test like this is of course not representative of the company as a whole or statistically relevant. But that's not the intention. One can easily see that it may give new cell members a frame of reference for the personal assessment they've received via their individual Q tests, and that may help them to open up to the idea that they have some developmental work to do. The stories of "old guys" Bert Stohr and Bernardus Venema, and "not so old guy" Casper van Dijke can be considered evidence that such work may indeed be effective, not just for themselves as individuals but also for the business cells as social and professional support systems.

Pizza or no pizza

'Is there vegetarian pizza?' Employeneur Berend van den Berg asks around in the bar area of TMC's headquarters, trying to be a good host to the guest from India. That night (October 30, 2019), the TMC Manufacturing Support cell had organized a "pizza session." This one was not just for cell members but also for potential new employeneurs and potential new clients. One such potential client is Lagom Automation, a recently started Dutch subsidiary of Compucare India Pvt. Ltd., an Indian producer of security and industrial automation equipment that wants to expand its activities to Europe. It turned out that there was indeed vegetarian pizza. With a piece of it in his hand, Lagom's representative, Karmit Goswami, explains how he became aware of this session. "As a company, we get assistance from the Brabant Development Agency [a public investment company and "growth accelerator" set up by the provincial and national government]. They connected us with TMC but also with the JADS Data Science Academy in Den Bosch and with the industrial VDL Group in Eindhoven." Goswami came to the meeting "to see if TMC could work for my company," he says.[10]

Pizza sessions are quite popular at TMC. They usually start at 5 pm, so right after work. The company pays for the pizzas, the employeneurs organize the sessions, either on a cell level or company-wide. The sessions can be initiated by anyone: from cell director to individual employee. They can focus on anything. Bernardus Venema organized a pizza session about digital technology (for beginners) and one about the Korean martial art of taekwondo; Bert Stohr did one about the Industry 4.0 movement; Mark Robinson, a British TMC employeneur, who we will meet in a little while, organized a session about presentation techniques.

Taking the initiative for a pizza session is highly appreciated, in both a social and financial sense: as an indication of your commitment to the company, it will have a positive impact on your annual evaluation and thus on your profit sharing percentage. On the other hand, if you don't like to participate in them or never organize one, you will not be blamed. Initially, Linda van Leuken, a 35-year-old chemical engineer who has been working for TMC since 2012, thought it might be held against her. "In the beginning, when I still was in the Chemical cell, not going would weigh on my mind. I felt a little obliged to go. I thought it was expected that I would. At TMC it is appreciated that you show yourself." Over time, she became more relaxed about this. When we talked with her in the fall of 2019, she gave two reasons why the pizza sessions "are not really my thing." First, she's a mother of two children, nine and ten years old, so the timing of the sessions is not very convenient for her. Second, she's not that interested in the more technical pizza sessions, about — say — capacitive micro-machined ultrasonic transducers. "I prefer things that can be explained in simple terms." She does like the competence group sessions with her cell (manufacturing support), though, because "then you are among like-minded people."[11]

On the other hand, pizza sessions may become the birthplace of a new venture.

Meet Mark Robinson, mathematician, 47 years old when we interviewed him in early 2019, originally from Devon, the United Kingdom, married to a Dutch lady and hence living in the Netherlands. For ten years he worked at three other consultancies, then he settled at TMC. He did projects at ASML, Philips Health Care and Liberty Global, UPC; all in all more than ten projects. "Right now, I'm doing my fifth project at ASML," he said. "I need the challenge and the change; once I know how things work, I get bored." Robinson belongs to the TMC Test & Integration cell, one of the newer ones. Like other seniors within TMC, he gradually grew into the role of team leader. "Right now I am an Agile 'scrum master' at ASML, for two teams." (within the Agile transformation method, a "scrum master" is primarily a facilitator and a coach). "We're even building a TMC Agile cell, that will be a kind of consultancy, to help clients build teams and give training courses, we already have a demand for that, it may become huge."[12]

Clearly, Mark is gifted with the entrepreneurial spirit TMC advocates and likes. In 2013, not long after he joined the company, he and his wife — who is a communications trainer — organized a session on how to "improve your presentation." That was a great success; around sixty people participated. Mark organized similar sessions, not just at TMC but also at ASML. After a TEDx talk at the High Tech Campus in Eindhoven in 2016, he began to receive invitations, and in 2017 he founded the Mark Robinson Training company. "TMC supported this move," he said, "and Thijs himself gave me personal advice." Now his training business takes up ten percent of his time and his work for TMC ninety percent. "I'd gradually like to shift that to forty-sixty," he said.[13]

Pillar 2: individual profit sharing

One might expect that a 59-year-old would choose security (the long-term relationship) as his favorite TMC pillar, but for Bernardus Venema, it is the profit sharing system and TMC's transparency about its fees and costs. "The profit share in your TMC income increases over time. Upon entering the company you may agree a profit share of — say — ten percent. If your annual evaluation turns out positive, you will go to maybe twelve percent. And so on. In my case it's gone up to thirty-eight percent. Each month I receive an Excel sheet with an overview of the fee TMC charges the client, the hours I worked, my fixed salary, my personal costs (like those for the use of a leased car), et cetera. What remains is the profit they made on me, and of that I get the thirty-eight percent. If I take a two-week vacation, there will be no profit sharing on those weeks. It's all very transparent, I can see exactly where the money is going."

This transparency appeals especially to foreigners who come to work for TMC. At the DNA Workshop of November 2019, which we visited earlier, Prenella Patterson from the New York office said she most of all loooved the profit sharing: "That was the main reason for me to say: sign me up!" Her French-speaking Belgian colleague Romain Meunier agreed: "TMC's transparency about its fees, salaries and profit is magnificent, I could hardly believe it. Money is not the most important thing for me, but it is nice to see how much the cost price is and how valuable you are for the company."

THE BONUSES
At TMC, every employeneur will be offered a bonus scheme, which is directly related to the gross margin the company generates on their consultancy fee. Bonuses vary from approximately ten to fifty percent. In 2017, for example, the company paid €35.5 million in wages and salaries, and €5.7 million in bonuses. This comes down to an average of sixteen percent. If social security premiums, leasing costs, pension costs and other costs are brought into the equation, the bonus percentage was 11.2 percent. The individual bonus level depends on the performance and seniority of the employeneurs, and on the amount of entrepreneurial risk they want to take, which makes it an instrument to stimulate both their engagement and their willingness to stay.[14]

Later on, in a Skype interview from France, Loïc le Mené, who runs TMC's Paris office, confirmed this. "Over here, the disruptive thing is the transparency, more than the individual profit sharing." In France, he explained, it is not done to talk about money and salaries.

"The other consultancies in France are playing with that. They try to hire people at a low cost and sell the service at higher cost. In between is a black box, and nobody, not even the managers, are aware of what stays in there."

When Danny Hameeteman made his acquaintance with the company in 2016, it was probably hard for him to choose which element of the TMC package he considered to be the best. He was twenty-four years old and had just acquired his master's degree in systems and control engineering (mechatronics) at the Delft University of Technology. During his studies, he had done an internship at Festo, a German producer of air-powered systems. "They had a small innovation task force which was developing bio-inspired mini robots, so in the shape of kangaroos, seagulls or ants. I wrote software for the robot ants to autonomously navigate, based on camera vision." He first talked with TMC at Delft University of Technology where the company presented itself during a recruitment event. What struck him most was the diversity of projects they had to offer and their emphasis on entrepreneurship — the latter in particular because he had tried and failed to set up a company during his study years.

What must have struck him too was that TMC offered him a contract despite the fact that the first client he went to for a job interview, rejected him. "I was in VIP for five months, which is pretty long, because the average is one month." In VIP? Yeah, in TMC lingo that stands for *vrij in project* (free in project, meaning: not currently working in a project). What does a young, not-yet-employeneur do in such a period? Plenty of things, Danny told us. "I polished my resume, visited colleagues at their jobs — for example at TNO, ASML, the Eindhoven University of Technology — took job interview training and began a project in The Entrepreneurial Lab."

Danny's package is based on a forty-hour working week, he told me when I interviewed him in early 2019. He didn't mention his profit sharing level but did mention the major elements in his annual assessment which would influence the percentage: things like his work experience, job performance, engagement with TMC (reflected by the number of Q meetings and pizza sessions he attended), and his use of his personal training and development budget.

Danny's first project was at the Dutch branch of Hyster Yale. This American manufacturer of forklifts and other material-handling equipment opened its first factory outside the USA in 1952 in the city of Nijmegen. The factory survived many economic crises and mainly produces big trucks, machines for lifting and moving heavy containers. "These are operated with joysticks," Danny explained, "which are connected to PLCs [programmable logic controllers]. Hyster wanted to move the operating system to a more flexible software platform, and I helped with that transfer."

He stayed almost one year at Hyster and then moved on to work in the "wafer stage control" systems group at ASML. Stages are tables on which silicon wafers are placed for processing. They have to be positioned very accurately and require advanced software control systems, which are able to send diagnostic data of deviations and errors from ASML machines at the clients' locations, anywhere in the world, to the company's service centers. There were about thirty people in the group he was part of, who had to solve difficult errors, build "proto-machines" (prototypes) and fix teething troubles in new product lines.

Apparently, he did well. In late 2018, ASML asked him to "convert" from a TMC contract to an ASML contract. "It was an interesting offer," Danny said. "But I declined because at TMC I would have more opportunities to develop myself." Which brings us to the next pillar.

Pillar 3: a long-term relationship

There are all kinds of routes to TMC. Danny Hameeteman met the company at a recruitment day at his university, Bert Stohr came over because TMC found him a job with less commuting time, Bernardus Venema got a tip to talk with TMC after he lost his job at Dräger. Every employeneur has a different story.

Meet Linda van Leuken. Yes, we've met her earlier but this time, we'll spend some more time with her. From 2001–2005 she studied chemical engineering at Fontys University of Applied Sciences in Eindhoven. After acquiring a bachelor's degree she took a job as a process engineer at a producer of beer filtration systems. Then she spent half a year — via a consultancy — at Philips Innovation Services, where she worked on non-reproducible photo-sensitive coatings. Then she got the opportunity of a fixed contract at chip manufacturer NXP. "I wanted to get married, have children, so a fixed contract would be better." She spent five years at NXP working on, among other things, complex oxidic thin films and helped bring a production idea to implementation. It was an instructive period but she wasn't very happy. "You had to know a lot about electronics; I didn't have that expertise and didn't want to have it either."[15]

Then, in 2012, after about five years at NXP, she was made redundant. And along came TMC. "I was looking for another job and found an opportunity at the Holst Center [a research center in Eindhoven, operated by TNO and the Flemish research group IMEC]. They wanted to develop flexible displays, using foils, which have to be put on silicon wafers. In this job I would be working with those foils." She applied, got the job. Then she was told: we can't hire you directly, it'll have to be via a consultancy. She could choose that consultancy herself. "Someone I knew at Philips advised me to choose TMC. I didn't know them, but I went to talk to them." Since she had already found a project, things went fast. "The TMC person I talked to knew me from my student days and they hired me very quickly." At that point she still hadn't the faintest idea what kind of company TMC was. She laughs out loud: "Of course they told me about their onboarding program and the coaching, et cetera. That was all fine with me, all I wanted was to go to work at the Holst Center."

That was seven years ago. She had left school seven years before and still wasn't sure whether she had made the right professional choices. As she put it in our interview: "I was still struggling to figure out what I really liked." To be sure, TMC invested quite a bit of energy into helping her. Troubled by this personal insecurity and by communication problems with colleagues at her workplace, she found support from her TMC coach — the second, because she didn't match very well with the first. Then, in 2015, when the Holst Center put her in a group where she wasn't happy, her account manager helped her find another project. "I went to a small manufacturer of lamination machines, IAI Industrial Systems. That was super."

What was also super was *The Goal: A Process of Ongoing Improvement*, by Eliyahu M. Goldratt. In this management book, written in a detective style, the main character is fighting for the survival of both his company and his marriage, and succeeds by thinking "out of the box." Goldratt used the story to explain his theory that every organization or process faces at least one constraint' that limits its further growth and development. In popular terms: every chain is only as strong as its weakest link. The challenge then is to deal with that constraint in a creative, ingenious way. *The Goal* was first published in 1984 and has since been reprinted many times, in many languages. It has been read by millions. The scene Linda liked best is the one in which the main character — named Alex Rogo — accompanies his son to a scout camp. The boys are walking to their destination and have to reach it before nightfall. Since the fastest boys are walking in front, the group repeatedly has to wait for the slowest one to catch up. Rogo first decides to reverse the walking order and puts the slowest one in front. Then he relieves this boy from his too-heavy backpack and distributes the contents among the others. As a result, not just the slow boy but the entire group speeds up and they reach their goal on time. "Eventually he used this method to improve the production processes in his company," Linda concludes her summary of the scene. While telling it, she has become fired with enthusiasm. "When I read that, I thought: now *this* is what I like. This is what I want, to observe and analyze and improve production systems."

When IAI offered her a job as a team leader of development, Linda felt that this would offer her the opportunity to do just what she wanted: observe, analyze and improve processes. So when IAI required that to get the job, she'd have to convert to a fixed contract, she did not hesitate. Even if TMC had invested a lot of support in her, she had to say, "Sorry, I'm leaving."

Only then did she discover the real meaning of the word constraint. The team leader job proved challenging, in a positive sense. But soon she found herself in the middle of a battle between some of her team members — male, some of them up to twenty years older than she was — and their manager, who was not a gifted communicator and had a tough style. Linda didn't particularly like his style either but agreed with his professional standards. However, the opposing team members succeeded in getting the manager replaced. "I was the team leader, but I was passed on the left and on the right." Things escalated due to different opinions on quality and, in the end, the new manager removed her from her position as a team leader.

At that point — three years after joining IAI — she decided to leave and return to TMC. "In that period of conflict, I really began to miss my coach and realize TMC's added value as a support system." Luckily, the company held no grudge against her for leaving. On the contrary, "They wholeheartedly welcomed me back." She asked Noortje van Boxtel, the director of TMC Manufacturing Support, if she could join that cell. TMC found her a job at Philips Research in Eindhoven that suits her well, she got back her old coach, she enthusiastically participated in a TMC introduction program — but for her it was more of a re-introduction program, of course.

When we interviewed her at Philips Research in 2019, she was helping this company to improve and standardize 'deposition tools' — equipment to depose ultrathin oxide or nitride layers on silicon wafers (for chip production) — by analyzing data collected during the deposition process. Like IAI four years before, Philips soon asked her to convert to a direct contract with them. This time, she refused. "My appreciation for TMC is very high now. The most important reason not to convert to a contract at Philips is the coaching TMC offers. I like that very much. Then there are the courses: I just have to indicate which course I want to do and I can do it. Plus, TMC has all kinds of activities that are fun." Not so much the pizza sessions but she does like the sports workshops. But the most important reason for her newfound loyalty is this: "TMC has helped me to develop a vision on what I want. I was always pleasing others and depended on confirmation from others: yes, you're doing well. But society doesn't always work that way, doesn't always give you that confirmation. So you have to learn how to be happy with who you are and what you are doing yourself. And they really helped me with that."

THE WAR FOR TALENT

As will be clear, Linda is not the only employeneur who has been offered a job by the client where she is placed. It happens to almost all employeneurs, all the time and at almost every client. That makes sense, and — whichever way one looks at it — it's unavoidable. The labor market is indeed a marketplace. Highly trained, highly qualified staff are always in high demand. High-tech companies in particular have to spend considerable amounts of time and money on their recruitment and retention tactics. Logically, they use consultancies as one of their recruitment channels.

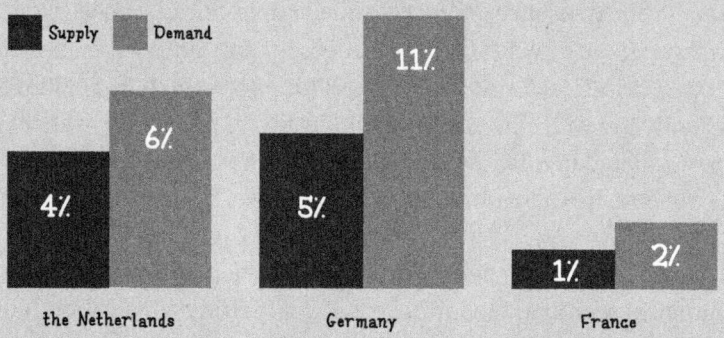

In this war for talent, TMC is not doing badly at all, even if the company doesn't impose non-competition clauses. Between 2014 and 2017, its inflow and outflow of employeneurs resulted in a churn rate of around 25 percent — which is way below average in this industry. In 2017, for example, the company hired 337 new members and saw 225 of them leave — resulting in net growth from 743 to 855 members. On average, around 30 percent of the employeneurs have been at TMC for three years. They move from project to project and hardly spend any time (a little over 4 percent) in between. Typical placements last around 13 months.[16]

Pillar 4: the YOUniversity

It wasn't until I began writing this section that I discovered the true intention of the term YOUniversity. This is what happened. I started scouring through my documentation to find a scene, a meeting or a venue which would best describe the TMC YOUniversity and its activities. I didn't find one. Then it dawned on me. The YOUniversity is not a physical university, it has neither a specific location nor a detailed curriculum. It is indeed what TMC claims it to be: a personalized development program. *The* YOUniversity does not exist, there are as many YOUniversities as there are employeneurs. To put it differently, TMC's employeneurs each have their own YOUniversity, their own, personal center of education, which they can fit up and organize the way they want and the way that suits them best.

TMC describes the concept of YOUniversity as a "continuous assessment of the employeneur's personal, professional and entrepreneurial development, beginning on day 1." That assessment starts with an Employeneur Analysis, on the basis of which the new employeneurs and their personal coaches create a personal development plan which in turn will act as a compass to guide them through their personal YOUrnies.

A PERSONAL BUDGET

Every TMC employeneur is awarded an annual budget of €2,000 to be spent in consultation with the cell director but basically at the individual's wants and requests. The budget may be used for hard skills education such as technical training or courses in, for example, designing experiments or project-based thinking and working, but is also available for the training of entrepreneurial skills such as presenting, networking and assertiveness.

After the initial assessment, YOUniversity continues, as do the employeneurs' YOUrnies through their career and life. All things considered, the concept includes the entire evaluation and support system that TMC has put in place for its employeneurs: the personal coaching (on a permanent basis, about once every seven weeks); the interactions in the Q meetings, competence groups and pizza sessions; a wide variety of internal and external training and courses; the mentoring of juniors by senior TMC members in their own business cells; the regular talks with account managers about ongoing and possible future projects; *and* the annual performance evaluations by their cell directors. All of these provide a constant feedback loop, one might say, which the employeneurs can put to their own benefit.

Pillar 5: The Entrepreneurial Lab

In September 2019, I visited yet another Q meeting, this one organized by TMC's Entrepreneurial Lab. Twenty-three people — among them four women — gathered in a conference room on the first floor of TMC's headquarters. Most of them were in their late twenties and early thirties. As is customary at TMC, everybody spoke English, even though the majority was Dutch. After a short explanation of the Microsoft Teams software, which the company had just started using as an internal communication tool, Lotte Geertsen, the director of The Entrepreneurial Lab (TEL), kicked off with some announcements. One was about a new start-up course for employeneurs who want to start their own company; another was that the employeneurs awards — intended as an extra incentive for promising projects — had been increased to €2,500 (the bronze award), €5,000 (silver) and €7,500 (gold).[17]

Then various teams gave an update on their projects. First up was the 3BEAM team, represented by employeneur Juan Sanchez Moreno. For the past 2.5 years, the seven members of this team had been working on an interactive light show, using colored light beams. On the one hand, it is an engineering project, involving sensors, lamps and software. But on the other hand it is an art project that aims to offer audience entertainment, optical illusions and a WOW experience.

In 2018 the team gave their first show during the GLOW lighting festival in Eindhoven (see QR code on p. 207 for video). Since then, they have developed the technology further. Drawing on a whiteboard, Juan explains how the system is now able to use the audience as a projection screen, thus increasing the feeling of interactivity. The inspiration for this development actually came from the visitors to one of the shows who began making photos of the light projections on people's faces.

The Entrepreneurial Lab, the company writes in one of its strategy documents, is a platform to "create and stimulate entrepreneurial behavior" and to "unlock out-of-the-box thinking." The concept arose in a conversation between Thijs Manders and consultant and organizational scientist Mathieu Weggeman, back in 2008. As

Manders and Weggeman remembered, the idea was to create "a safe environment for engineers to develop their entrepreneurship, in multidisciplinary groups," and a place for employeneurs who were temporarily without a project to work on their own ideas.[18]

The lab is a physical playground (a room filled with tools and equipment), a social environment in which "employeneurs can share a joint passion for innovation, technology and creativity" and an experimental environment, which allows the employeneurs "to experience first-hand what it takes to become an entrepreneur." Its mission is to develop "technology-based solutions for real problems and societal challenges." The lab provides not just physical tools but also financial means — development budgets at various stages, the project awards mentioned above and personal awards — and entrepreneurial coaching/guidance. TMC clearly regards it as a showcase: the lab is located in a corner of the ground floor of its headquarters and is the first thing visitors see when they walk towards to the building from the parking garage.

At the evening I attended, seven projects presented their updates — some were still in their early stages, others had suffered setbacks and delays. The 3BEAM project could of course claim some success (though not yet commercially) and one — Throwabot — in fact seemed to be attracting some interest from outside investors.

The leading man of the Throwabot team is young Danny Hameeteman (whom we already met in the section about individual profit sharing). He gave an update too. He and his team had been working on this project for about three years now. They got the original idea when they read that the Dutch Navy was looking for a company that could develop a reconnaissance robot for use in the Red Sea area near Somalia. The Dutch were participating in the international effort to protect merchant ships against pirates. A camera-equipped robot that could be thrown onto a hijacked vessel — from a helicopter or from another ship — might be helpful. Danny and his colleague figured that a small, robust, throwable, remote-controlled robot might be useful to inspect other dangerous places too — think of burning buildings or suspicious packages in railway stations. When I interviewed Danny in early 2019 his team had grown to six. Since

The throwabot is a light, disposable robot

to be thrown onto a ship

or inside a building

It has camera vision and audio

so that risks can be detected from a safe distance

the start, TMC had contributed €12,000 as a development budget, which the team had managed to increase by winning a bronze project award. During his September 2019 update, Danny revealed that the Throwabot model had been developed far enough to start thinking about a business plan and about attracting private investors. For the business plan, the team had been seeking advice from the (publicly funded) Brabant Development Agency. They had also had a first meeting with an investment company that was now considering accepting them into their accelerator program. Admittedly, these were just the first, cautious steps towards commercialization, production and a start-up company. Nevertheless, the project was alive and moving forward, and somewhere during Danny's presentation TEL director Lotte Geertsen revealed that the Dutch Ministry of Defense was actually considering a financial participation (in early 2020 the Throwabot project received a golden TMC Employeneurs Award).

If The Entrepreneurial Lab teaches TMC's employeneurs anything it is that developing an idea into a product and a company is not an easy road. It requires a lot of hard work, determination and resilience. Erik Hermans, for example, wanted to develop a passive filter system to catch microfibers in waste water of — for example — washing machines. He assembled a team, but one by one, the members left TMC and he had to build a new one. When asked for the lessons learned from this Fiber Fighter project during the September 2019 update meeting, he reacted (and drew laughter) by answering: "Don't leave TMC" and "keep your project documentation well organized and transferable." Because the first team fell apart and because its documentation had been chaotic, the new team had to start developing the filter all over again, Erik more or less admitted. At the end of his update, one of his TMC colleagues innocently asked: "What will you do with the microfibers your filter is catching?" His answer was honest but he clearly felt somewhat embarrassed: "We haven't thought about that yet."

Perhaps one of the nicest features of The Entrepreneurial Lab is that it allows TMC's employeneurs to dream and explore their ideas, without anyone commenting beforehand that "this is impossible." Consider the Allergique project, conceived by Bram Pape and Evelyn Blocken. They thought it would be great for people with allergies — of whom there are a lot — to have a wearable test kit, one that you can put in your purse or even your pocket. With such a kit these people could walk into any restaurant, anywhere in the world without having to worry about a possible attack on their health and their well-being. The idea came up at the end of 2018 and in 2019 it was approved as a TEL project, meaning that Bram and Evelyn received a modest initial development budget. When Bram gave an update at the September TEL meeting, he clearly had had a few reality checks. First of all, the Allergique project no longer aims to develop a test kit. The goal is much more limited and now concerns an app on which users should be able to see allergy information from the restaurant they're about to enter. This would require, of course, that restaurants feed that information into the system, on a daily basis. Bram admitted: "Our survey showed that only twenty-five percent of restaurants are interested," clearly not a promising number.

ENTREPRENEURIAL SPIRIT A1

A TMC member who certainly has that spirit is Jaap van der Heijden. His project has never been an official TEL project, but entrepreneurial it is and TMC has given him all the space and support he needed to get it off the ground. We met Jaap in October 2019, when he gave a presentation during the pizza session of the Manufacturing Support cell, described earlier. Jaap joined TMC in 2017 and had already tried to set up several start-ups around a variety of services, ranging from web design to business intelligence. When we met, Jaap worked four days per week as a project leader at a Bosch subsidiary in the city of Tilburg — some thirty kilometers northwest of Eindhoven. The fifth day is for his company Superdoos, in English: Super Box. Although it delivers cardboard boxes for packaging on demand, it is not a production company but an ordering and delivery system. Superdoos has also not invented or developed its boxes; Jaap uses the American FEFCO-type foldable boxes and has them made by producers in the Netherlands, Belgium and Germany. His focus is on the business-to-business market, with clients ordering two hundred to five thousand boxes. On Jaap's website, they can choose from a variety of types, indicate the exact sizes they desire, get a price indication and order. The system behind the website forwards this information directly to one of the manufacturers who will immediately start producing and arranging delivery.

During the pizza session, Jaap faced some tough questions about the sustainability of his business, which of course rests mainly on the optimization of logistic processes. What was his competitive advantage? And wasn't his business model easy to copy? Jaap indeed seemed to realize that, if he wants his business to become a success, he will need to do more than simply move boxes from producers to customers. He will have to offer true added value. One way to do that, he suggested, might be to offer clients the option to have their own logos and designs printed on their boxes. As yet, he hadn't found a suitable machine, so he had approached — yes! — Entrepreneurial Lab director Lotte Geertsen to discuss the possibility of developing such a machine. To be continued... hopefully for Jaap.

CHAPTER 4

THE PILOTS

"If you treat people as employeneurs they will start to behave like employeneurs"

(EMMANUEL MOTTRIE, TMC CEO)

CREATE YOUR DESTINY

The eye opener

Like most TMC employeneurs, Bernardus Venema is very positive about having a personal coach. "Usually they have both an engineering background and a background in the social sciences. They know how to hold up a mirror to you. That can be very refreshing, very interesting," he said. "These meetings often bring me eye openers about how I deal with my life and my work." For example? "At one of the company's I worked for, I had a very irritating colleague. Every now and then I had to attend meetings where he was too. I was extremely annoyed by him, but I couldn't avoid those meetings. So I talked to my coach about him, and he eventually brought to the surface why I became so irritated. When I returned home that day, my wife said: what happened, you look so happy? And I was happy. It had been a wonderful session. After that, I never was irritated with the guy anymore, the sting had been taken out, it wasn't important anymore, I couldn't care less. That's the beauty of the coaching process. Now I don't even remember what this irritation was all about."[1]

His colleague Bert Stohr describes the sessions with his coach as "intimate." "Coaching is a very personal thing. Whether it's successful or not depends on the interaction and on the personal 'click' you have with him of her. My experiences with coaches are both negative and positive. If the interaction doesn't work well, the frequency of the sessions will go down, the periods in between will lengthen, until you think: let's just forget about it. But if the 'click' is good, the sessions will find a natural frequency and you will look forward to the next one. And you can always ask for an extra session if you get stuck in some situation or maybe feel uncomfortable with yourself and want to talk about it."[2]

El Patrón

People can feel uncomfortable about almost anything. On one of his jobs, Bernardus Venema was complimented for being such a nice boss. Most of us would say "thank you." Not Bernardus. "I didn't want to be a boss at all. When I talked to my coach about this, he began to explore the issue deeply: why not? And I said: I prefer to be regarded as someone who helps the people on the shop floor improve their work. 'Well,' said my coach, 'whether you like it or not, apparently you do have qualities that make people see you as a nice boss.' And I said: that may be the case, but I wouldn't want TMC to send me to a client as a department head. I don't think that would make me happy." During the session Venema and his coach decided that he would talk to the workers. "I told them: your boss is upstairs, he arranges your evaluation sessions and other HRM-like things. I don't have anything to do with that. On the contrary. I'm your patron, I try to make sure that you're not bothered by the people from upstairs who give you all kinds of incomprehensible orders. And I'm here to give you information — if you need that — or maybe arrange training. OK, they said, in that case we'll call you *El Patrón*. I liked the mafia sound of that, so I accepted. When I entered the clean room the next day, there was a label on one of the hooks on which you hang your jacket: reserved for *el patrón*."

The pursuit of happiness

Now meet Ignacio Vazquez. A big, boyish, sinewy guy with dark eyes and a firm handshake, dressed in a casual t-shirt. We met him in August 2019, in a building rented by ASML at the Flight Forum, near Eindhoven Airport. He leads the way through the building's lunch area, which is packed with other people of his age, both men and women, all engaged in lively chatter. Very animated atmosphere indeed. We move on to the second floor, where Ignacio has reserved a quiet room for the interview.[3]

Ignacio is 30 years old. He was born and raised in Mexico and still has a Mexican passport. After he had obtained a bachelor's degree in mechatronics in 2011, he worked for a Mexican subsidiary of Continental, a German producer of tires and braking systems. After a while he decided that, if he wanted to do really interesting projects, he needed a master's degree. Plus he decided that he wanted to do the necessary studies abroad. He sent applications to ten universities, was accepted by eight and chose Eindhoven Technical University. He obtained his master's degree in two years. Then he returned to Mexico. The government had paid his scholarship on the condition that "you do something for society in return." In Ignacio's case that meant being a high school teacher for half a year.

Then he received a phone call from the Netherlands. One of his former university teachers had a job offer for him. It turned out to be a job at TMC for a project at the DAF manufacturing company (which is owned by the American PACCAR group). TMC was not an unfamiliar name for him. "When I was still studying, I had already met one of their account managers."

In 2016, he returned to the Netherlands, this time for work. That was different.

"When I had been at Eindhoven University of Technology, it was for a limited period. Plus I had student friends. So I lived in a bubble. But when I began to work at DAF, I landed in the real Netherlands. DAF was extremely Dutch, in my department there were about a hundred people and maybe three foreigners. So starting to work there was a culture shock. And an age shock: most of the engineers were over fifty, when they left work, they went to their families and social circles. They had their own lives, of which I knew nothing. For me, it was different. I went to my house to eat and sleep, and then went back to work again. I wasn't living." He struggled a lot during that first year. But not entirely on his own, thanks to the coach TMC had offered him, who helped him find his way. "The talks with my coach in that period were mainly about that, about the personal side of my life, about building a new life in a new country."

At the end of his first year, an unpleasant surprise brought him new experiences with the TMC model. "DAF ran into financial and internal problems, and in December I found out — through office gossip — that they would not renew the consultancy contracts." The situation made him angry. "But it was then that I got to know TMC as a company and as a team, and found out that it was not just any consultancy. They began giving me tips, exposed me to other TMC people and offered me their network to find a new client." Which became ASML, where he moved to in early 2018 and still was when we met him (he is in the overlay control department, which develops highly specialized computer applications for the pattern-to-pattern alignment in the manufacture of silicon wafers).

During his three working years in the Netherlands, Ignacio has learned many things, about TMC, about building a life and about himself. When he came in 2016, as a 27-year-old, he was very conscious that his engineering skills had attracted attention. He was quite brilliant. Why else would he have been offered a job in the Netherlands? Yet his main discovery about himself in these years is not related to his engineering expertise, his mathematical skills or his professional development. It is a personal thing. As he put it, "I am very much oriented towards interacting with other people." In his job at ASML he has an intermediary role. "I'm in between the physicists and the software engineers." He gets interaction, yes, "But here there's just too much of it. I'm working with ten different teams. If I have a question, there are three hundred people I can choose from to get the answer. But I don't get to *know* anyone. And that is something I need in order to be happy."

This personal need has become so important that he decided to decline ASML's offer of a transfer from TMC to them. "It was a significant offer. I would have had a challenging job that requires a lot of knowledge and high-level communication. But at the end of the day I don't think I will make a difference, that what I would do will really change anything. If I would leave that job, someone else would simply pick it up and continue. Nothing would change." So now what? "I guess I have to find another client."

What Ignacio really wants, he says, is a sense of fulfillment on a personal level. His awareness of that need was stimulated by his adjustment problems, during his first TMC year at DAF, but also by TMC itself. "When I was working at DAF, managers of TMC approached us — a few foreigners — and said: we are getting a lot of employeneurs from other countries, that's very nice, they work, sometimes they even bring their families, but once they are working at a client, we don't really do anything with them. We want to do better. Please talk about it and let us know what you think. We were four and we organized a pizza session." To their surprise, some sixty people showed up. "A very strong reaction and many volunteered to do all kinds of things." Ignacio had found a mission. Together with seven other TMC expats he set up a TMC expat community.

As he talks about this community, it's obvious that this project is close to his heart. He becomes more lively and radiates enthusiasm. "We started activities to help people coming to work for TMC to integrate in the Netherlands. We began organizing sessions for them, their partners, sometimes their families, to explain what it is like to live here. We had a very motivated group of people. This was a volunteer thing but we spent several hours per week, thinking, planning, contacting people, to get money to organize. And that was what I had missed during my work here."
Thus began his shift towards the pursuit of happiness.

"This journey never ends"

When we interviewed Ignacio in August 2019, he was still actively engaged in TMC's expat community. "We have monthly events, social things, board game evenings, potluck dinners, visits to sites like the Kinderdijk windmills. We rented a bus to take families with children to the miniature town of Madurodam. We organize walking tours to cities like Den Bosch and Utrecht, places that are nice to know about. We always try to make these trips interesting for our Dutch colleagues too, so we include a learning aspect and get guides. We don't want this group to be only for expats, we want to mix, interact with the Dutch."

While setting up TMC's expat community, he discovered himself as an organizer. "As you know, TMC is opening offices everywhere, Belgium, Italy, Spain, France," he said. "About a year ago I was talking to my manager at TMC. I said: I hear they are opening new offices; it would be nice to have an overview and organize something for the expats there. He said, okay, and I sent an email to the CEO of Belgium [Emmanuel Mottrie, who later became the group CEO] and said it would be very nice if you can come here to explain to anyone who wants to join what is happening with this expansion of TMC, and within in the hour he sent an answer: 'Great idea. When?' One line, ha-ha." At some point he realized: "When I organize something, people will follow me." Now he proudly writes in his resume: "I am able to build connections and inspire a team of people to work towards a common goal." TMC continued to actively stimulate this, he said. "My manager at TMC encourages me to continue doing these things, but not only by saying, good work. When the time is there for the yearly evaluation, it counts, strongly. And it is valued in money. So I gained significantly larger raises than if I hadn't been so engaged in organizing these things. It felt really good. It is something I found out that I liked, found out that I was good at."

As a result of this rewarding — both personally and financially — learning experience Ignacio decided that in his work too, he needed to "include people things." And he talked about this with the growing number of TMC account managers and cell directors he had met through his social activities in the TMC expat community. Somewhere in 2019 one of them asked him if he would like to coach students at Eindhoven University of Technology, for a few hours per week. He said "yes" and started this coaching in February 2020.

He also talked with his coach, of course. His second one. "The discussions with my first coach were: what does living in the Netherlands mean for me? With my new coach it is about the leadership things, about trying to pull people together and how to do that. I classify myself more as introvert than extrovert, so I had to learn to balance my energy to interact with many people and still be able to make strong connections. I had to learn to open up more, to empathize. This journey never ends, and with my coach we always have some topics to talk about."

Has he found happiness? "I feel at home here now," he says. "I have friends, a network of acquaintances, which is very important. I am very much aware that there are still many things I don't know, but I do see a lot of potential. And yes, I do have the feeling that I am making a difference, however small it may be. And that is a precious feeling."

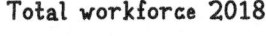

Total workforce 2018

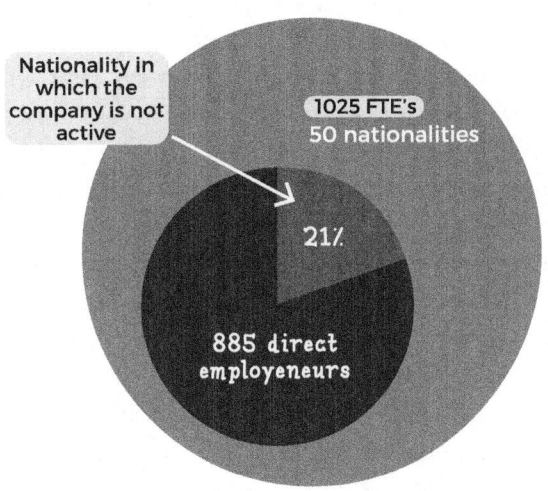

Nationality in which the company is not active

1025 FTE's
50 nationalities

21%

885 direct employeneurs

Six months after the interview, the good feeling continues. When we ask him via email how he's doing, he replies: "I'm posted at DAF again, now as a senior engineer, and at Eindhoven University of Technology, as an innovation coach. I am leading a TMC team within my cell, became the CEO of a start-up for about six months (with the support from my account manager) and got accepted for a two-year management program at the Massachusetts Institute of Technology in Boston. I'm really happy with how things turned out. The offer from ASML [which he rejected] even seems a bit funny now. My conditions (salary and such) are better than what ASML offered me, I have the project coaching students at the university, which is amazingly satisfying. I'm working on formalizing a collaboration between TMC and a consortium of universities to carry out medical research, and I'm lined up for a promotion this year. I mean, things are looking great!"

I DON'T NEED ALL THAT

When new employeneurs meet their first coach, they set out on the initial assessment, described in broad terms earlier (and in more detailed terms later). TMC regards this assessment and coaching trajectory as an offer you *can* refuse — it is not presented until after the contract has been signed. One who did indeed initially reject it was Linda van Leuken, whom we met before. When she first joined TMC in 2012, she accepted the coach but skipped the personal development plan exercise. "That was terrible, I didn't know what to write, I guess I just wasn't open to it," she said seven years later, when we interviewed her. What didn't help was that she was assigned a coach who was relatively inexperienced and didn't know how to handle her. All her efforts to push Linda into cooperation backfired and even hardened Linda's resistance. "I didn't want to accept anything from her." After she had been assigned a new coach — at her own request — that resistance quickly melted away, however. The new coach "respected me, and when she disagreed with me, she wouldn't say it but ask me questions that gave me pause for thought." Small wonder that upon her return to TMC in 2018 she immediately asked this second coach — the same one who had helped her "develop a vision on what I want" — to assist her once again.[4]

For Freek van Bedaf, who developed the TMC assessment test and the permanent coaching model, this story is not uncommon. "Many techies at first say: I don't need all that. But in hindsight, they will admit: now that I've experienced it, coaching was a great help." Linda van Leuken agrees. "When I started at TMC, I was still young and my communication skills weren't very well-developed. I talked about that with my coach; she gave me feedback and suggestions about how to handle certain situations. Over the years, my self-confidence has increased hugely."[5]

Techies primarily love to talk tech. All TMC employeneurs do. Ask them about their projects and all you have to do is lean back and record their stories — until you get tired, because they won't.

Tech talk (1): hydrogen fuel cells

Meet Ronald Cornelissen, born in 1969, so 50 years old when we meet him in his home in a suburb of the city of Nijmegen (some sixty kilometers from Eindhoven). He was trained as a chemical engineer at Fontys University of Applied Sciences (Eindhoven) but over the years develop a wide range of expertise. Today, he describes himself as an "all-round process/product engineer." He joined TMC in October 2012 after three direct contracts at other companies. Why TMC? Simply because he had lost his job. It was a case of bad luck. In 2010, he had decided to follow his wife. He had been working at Océ Technologies for fourteen years. Meanwhile his wife, who is an astronomer, was offered a job at Astron, the Netherlands Institute for Radio Astronomy. Océ is located in Venlo, in the south of the Netherlands; Astron in Dwingeloo, two hundred kilometers to the north of Venlo. So Ronald left Océ and took a job at Philips' Consumer Lifestyle Products division in Drachten, which is only a fifty minute drive north from Dwingeloo. That didn't last long. In 2011, his wife got another job, now at Radboud University Nijmegen, about 150 kilometers back south again. Ronald followed once more and found a job at Nedstack, a hydrogen fuel cell producer, spun off from Akzo Nobel in 1999 and located in Arnhem, some twenty kilometers from Nijmegen. Unfortunately, the economic circumstances — in the wake of the 2008–2009 financial crisis — were not very favorable, and the project he was working on didn't get off the ground. So in 2012, he found himself jobless.[6]

His setback didn't last long. On a nice day in summer, he went to the Eindhoven Students Gliding Club, of which he was a member, where he met a female TMC account manager. When he told her a little about his professional career, she asked him to send his resume. "She called me back fifteen minutes after receiving it," Ronald remembers. "And yeah, I know, my professional profile is quite unique."

When he gets into the details of that profile, it quickly becomes clear that he is not exaggerating. During his first years at Océ he worked on rubber and acquired a patent (as a co-inventor) on a new method for synthesizing it. Then he was put in charge of a project for the improvement of a manufacturing process and helped set up two new plants. At Philips, he (co-)developed a new (cold) metal forming technique for the manufacturing of rotating shaving heads. At Nedstack, he worked on manufacturability and ramping up production of hydrogen fuel cells.

Tech Talk (2): the push-belt

When Ronald joined TMC, Stijn Huijbers, the account manager of the manufacturing support cell at that time, immediately had a project for him at Bosch Transmission Technology, which is located in Tilburg. "During the interview they presented me with some technical problems," he recounts. Apparently, they liked the way he handled those. They immediately accepted him. He explains what Bosch Transmission is all about. Originally this subsidiary of the German Bosch group was a Dutch company. It was set up in 1958 by the founder of DAF Trucks, Hub van Doorne, who wanted to develop a continuous variable transmission (CVT) for passenger cars. Van Doorne first invented a system with a rubber drive belt running between pulleys with — automatically adjusting — conical sheaves. Later, the company changed this rubber belt for a steel push-belt. Ronald explains in clear terms how the steel links in the push-belt press together and thus create a much higher torque in transferring the energy from the engine to the drive axle than a drive belt, which uses tractive force. After Bosch acquired CVT in 1995, the German group continued improving the push-belt as a key element in one of its automatic transmission systems (Bosch produces other systems as well). Today it manufactures millions of them in factories in the Netherlands (Tilburg), Vietnam (Ho Chi Minh City) and Mexico (San Luis Potosi).[7]

Push-belts consist of hundreds of steel links, strung along high alloy steel rings. Ronald's job at Bosch was to simplify the production process of the steel links. His innovative contribution resulted in two more patents, one for laser welding and one for a technology to punch the links — at high speed, in high numbers — from very thin steel sheets. Bosch was happy with him. "My contract was supposed to last one to two years but was extended by follow-up projects to over four years." Yet, in 2017 he decided to leave. He and his wife had young children and he wanted to spend more time at home (and less on the seventy kilometer commute between Nijmegen and Tilburg).

Leaving Bosch also meant leaving TMC, which wasn't able to offer him a job close to home. But after an intermediate — and technologically not very interesting — year at a manufacturer of cargo securing materials, he returned. On his own initiative. MSD, the pharmaceutical giant, offered him a project at their Dutch animal health subsidiary, which mainly produces vaccines and is located in Boxmeer, a mere thirty kilometers from his home. It sounded like a great opportunity, in which he would be able to employ both his chemical engineering background and his experience with production systems and production technologies. But it would also involve a lot of travel (not so much commuting but job-related, international travel). In case he didn't like it, however, he wanted some form of security. "I decided that I wanted to do this with TMC. They hadn't been able to give me a project close to home, but in general their jobs are nice. So if things wouldn't work out well at MSD...Plus, they offer the personal development tools." TMC was glad to see him come back. He started working at MSD Animal Health in November 2018. First, he helped set up a tracking and tracing system for MSD's animal medicines, for use on the Chinese market. Then, he became responsible for designing and building a new vaccine packaging line as part of a factory. Both were challenging jobs, and at the time of writing he's still working at MSD.

Tech talk (3): high-speed packaging

When meeting Ronald Cornelissen, one's first impression is that of a very friendly, rather shy person. Not very talkative. But first impressions are deceptive, and as soon as the conversation turns to technical and practical issues, there he goes. Casper van Dijke, on the other hand, whom we met earlier at Demcon, the medical isotope producer in Eindhoven, is a fast and lively speaker by nature. If you want to get *him* started, you better bring a recording device, so you can replay his stories at reduced speed.[8]

His first job — back in 2005 and not via TMC — was at Houdijk Holland, a manufacturer of transport systems. "Imagine," he says, "a rusk in round slices. The slices are baked in an oven and need to be packaged. So you need a system to transport the rusk slices to the packaging machine, include a buffering area, make rolls of thirteen slices, and make sure the final one is put in the package upside down. I had to talk to the salespeople and the engineers, and then make a layout of a production line that could do this, including quality control with high-speed cameras. Chocolate chip cookies would pass the camera one by one, rice waffles in bulk. I did that for eight months. I learned a lot but I wanted to learn faster, so I did all kinds of things on the side; for example, I documented some of their standard systems, which they knew of course how to build but had never put on paper. And I worked a bit on their website."

After a seven month journey to Asia with his girlfriend — the trip included a ride on the Trans-Siberian railway from Moscow to Beijing, in the middle of winter — and a short stint at a manufacturer of packaging systems for the pharmaceutical industry, he wound up at ASML. "I became a member of a tooling team. We developed parts for their EUV machines, in which they use extreme ultraviolet light with very short wavelengths and mirrors in a vacuum to create very precise chip details. At the time (2009) they were developing the first models of those machines." What did they look like? "Imagine a machine of eight meters in length, four in width and four in height, with all kinds of additional equipment. The frames in those machines can weigh a couple of tons. We had to develop tools to put those frames into position inside the machine, and tools for the mechanics to be able to work on them. My team built a kind of lifting bridge to hang a frame on, so the mechanics could reach the various components from all sides. To construct that, you need to figure out what such a piece of equipment must be able to do: how high it must be able to lift, at which angle it should turn, et cetera."

Tech talk (4): high-intensity electronic particle beams

Casper's second project was at the Dutch subsidiary of Omron, a Japanese producer of programmable logistic controllers (PLCs), controlling devices which often co-operate with sensors and are an integral part of many automated production systems. Casper: "A PLC is a small box with all sorts of input and output ports, which connect to sensors and motors. They are very reliable and carry simple software, they basically always work. But over the last fifteen years, many manufacturers have started using industrial PCs, which have more complex and extensive software and allow for more flexible programming. Now the Japanese like security, so Omron has devised a PC with two cores: one flexible and one PLC. So if the PC crashes, the PLC will make sure that the production system keeps going. Now my job was to develop the shell." He's very proud of that shell. Its design won him two prestigious awards, both of which he mentions on his resume: the iF Design Award and the Reddot Award. "Omron wanted a flexible, modular and sturdy design," he explains. "Some clients want a fast version, others a slower one; some want a thin version, others a thicker one. We could deliver it 'built to order,' in a million different versions." He shows a picture on his computer screen. The shell has the shape of a shoebox. "There are six or seven patented components in it," he says. "And the final design is very close to my original concept. I'm very proud of it."

His latest project is probably the most technologically advanced project he has worked on in his entire fourteen-year career. In late 2017, he indicated to TMC that he was ready for another project, and in January 2018 TMC offered him one at Demcon, the medical equipment manufacturer he had also worked for in 2012–2014. This time they had what he calls "a crazy project": manufacturing medical isotopes. Such isotopes are radioactive fluids with low radiation levels, which are injected into a person's body for diagnostic scanning purposes — usually related to cancer. Their production requires specialized nuclear reactors, which of course also produce nuclear waste. Again, Casper is eager to explain: "We are working with a technology that was first described in the 1930s/1940s. Later experiments have delivered proof for it, but they didn't aim for commercialization. Now it is being adapted to create isotopes that do not require nuclear fission." The new technology uses electronic particle beams "to transform a non-active isotope into an active one." According to Casper, someone at ASML — which was developing this technology for its chip production systems — realized that high-intensity electronic particle beams might be applied to create medical isotopes. Casper van Dijke: "So they formed a consortium with some other companies, called it Lighthouse, and asked Demcon to help build such a system."

Demcon, in turn, asked Casper — via TMC — to join the team. Which he did. "It's mechanics with a lot of thermal challenges, because it's very hot — which Demcon is good at — and then there's a part that has to do with radiation and shielding, which Demcon is not familiar with. Anyway, it sounded like an interesting co-operation and an interesting project to me." That was two years ago. So how are things working out? "The project turned out to be quite a challenge," Casper says. "It's much more complex than we thought at the start. On some aspects, we need more expertise, in physics and chemistry, for example. What we are doing now is fundamental research and product development at the same time." He expressed some doubt as to whether there would be a role for him in a prolonged research phase (apparently, the project continued to fascinate him, at the time of writing — May 2020 — he was still working at Demcon).

Tech talk (5): layer deposition

Linda van Leuken, too, lightens up when she goes into the details of her work. One such moment is when she remembers her time at IAI, which — as described earlier — was difficult in terms of team relations but exciting in terms of technical challenges. "Their lamination machines are being used for personalized identification materials like passports and the like. Your photo is put on them, your name, security features. They develop the processes for that. That's cool! Before I came there, I had been wondering what would make me happy in my work. At IAI I discovered: what makes me happy is to see the finished product." It's no longer just that, the scope of her fascination has broadened to the point that even the analysis of production data — her present job — can enthuse her. "They [the client she was working for at the time of the interview, Philips Research] want more control over the layer deposition process [of their silicon wafer machine]. So I try to find out why layers that should be 100 nanometers thick sometimes are 110, despite unchanged machine settings. Could that variation be caused during maintenance? Maybe our measurements are not correct? Are there any differences in the way the operators handle the machine?" She loves that kind of detective work. "I'm totally happy. I try to involve everybody in my analyses: the engineers, maintenance people, operators. For the

maintenance people it was nice to hear that these thickness varia-
tions were not caused by them but by measurement errors. And if I
can show them that finding a solution to such a recurring error might
reduce the machine's downtime by ten percent, they are of course
very happy with that."[9]

Finding direction ...

...in a technological sense doesn't seem to pose a problem for TMC's
techies. All of our interviewees have taken additional courses. Interestingly, courses to acquire additional technological expertise
are in the minority. Most were to learn about and develop skills in
issues like general management (lean management, value stream
mapping), project management, project design, team leadership,
effective leadership, et cetera (even learning new languages and
improving one's foreign language skills is quite popular). This
illustrates their awareness that they *are* indeed on a journey, and
that they themselves have a major influence on where that journey
will take them. In many cases: a long way. Ronald Cornelissen, the
chemical engineer, started working in 2001 and now designs and develops entire factories in a team. Mark Robinson, the mathematician,
has been professionally active for just under two decades, started
out punching programming code and developed into a team leader,
"Agile scrum master," presentation coach and entrepreneur. Ignacio
Vazquez, the mechatronics engineer, obtained his master's degree
just four years ago and just recently returned to university as an innovation coach. Bert Stohr, the precision mechanics engineer, started
work (in 1990) as a product designer, then developed into a systems
architect, and for the last seven years acted as a leader of new product introduction projects. Bernardus Venema, the electronics engineer, set out as a designer of machine control systems. Gradually,
he developed an interest in production systems. Then his attention
shifted to people. In his spare time, he became a physics teacher. At
work, he started training operators and writing instructions for the
operation of newly developed high-tech machinery. Chemical engineer Linda, to mention just one more TMC techie, clearly encountered some difficult challenges along her fourteen-year professional
journey. But with some books, coaching and help from her TMC
managers, she too found direction.

Which is of course what TMC's YOUrney concept is all about: career development for engineers and technical people requires a lot of attention to their "soft skills" and their personal development. Time to take a closer look at the 5Qs.

| INSIDE EMPLOYENEURSHIP THEORY

The groundwork

> What is employeneurship? This is what TMC writes on its website:
>
> "Employeneurship is about thinking and acting like an entrepreneur, with the added security of employment."
>
> "But more than anything it is a guarantee for **continuous development** and the opportunity to really be fully responsible for **the direction of your career**."

The company explicitly connects the term to its own concept of career development and its five-pillar business model. But of course you know that already. The previous pages were all about this view and how it works out in TMC's practice.

Originator Freek van Bedaf has a slightly different focus. His Pontes Group describes employeneurship as:

> "A **mindset** that places confidence in the increase of happiness, success and satisfaction in life and work when someone is making him- or herself responsible for his or her own development. Not solely taking on easy challenges but also being able to take on obstructive patterns and obstacles."
>
> "A set of effective **behavioral patterns**, a structure, a method to be able to obtain personal development or the development of corresponding organizations."

With this description, Pontes looks at employeneurship from a psychological point of view: as both a mindset and a behavioral pattern. The group explicitly stresses the balance between work and personal life. And it puts employeneurship in a historical context: it can be regarded as "a display of the evolution of the motivation of the (working) human and its changing work relations." Put simply: it is a social innovation.

How did Van Bedaf develop these ideas? When I interviewed him, he summarized, "In the early TMC days, we started with the idea: we're going to deploy techies with soft skills. I did some research, adopted Howard Gardner's multiple intelligence theory, added theories about motivation and ended up with the 4Qs." Or rather 5Qs, because the four come together in XQ, executional intelligence, which Pontes describes as, "The internal dedication and discipline to develop your ideas, goals and plans and transform them into real results." In plain English: the ability to walk your talk.

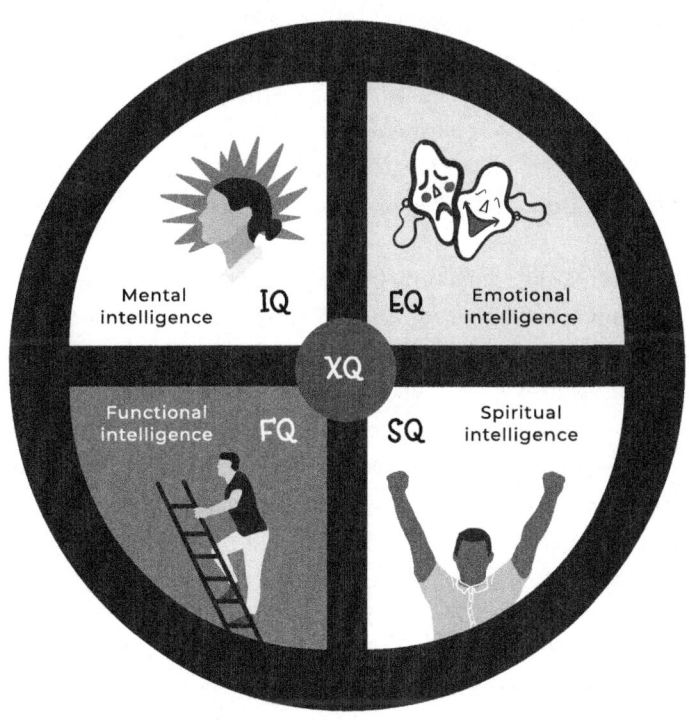

Van Bedaf's summary is correct but somewhat too modest. His developmental work started around 2010, after TMC's assessment division had been split off, put on its own feet and renamed Pontes — the Latin word for bridges. It took him around fifteen years.

First, he compiled a body of knowledge based on psychological, sociological and organizational concepts and theories developed since the 1950s.

The locus of control

A central one was the "locus of control" theory. According to the American psychologist Julian Rotter, who came up with this theory in 1954, people can be put on a spectrum with, at one end, those who believe that they can control their own lives and, at the other end, those who believe that their lives are predominantly controlled by external forces. The first have a strong internal locus of control; the latter a strong external locus of control. In the 1960s, other American psychologists — among whom was the famous Alfred Bandura — built on Rotter's ideas to develop a theory of social learning. Supporters of this theory rejected the suggestion made by behaviorist B.F. Skinner that all learning is simply the result of positive and negative stimuli (reward and punishment). Instead, they felt, learning should be seen as an active cognitive process which involves observation and interpretation, and takes place in a social context.[10]

Rotter wasn't Van Bedaf's only inspiration. He leaned on a wide range of other studies and theories, among which were Victor Vroom's landmark study *Work and Motivation* (1964); the motivation model Porter and Lawler based on Vroom's ideas (1968); John Kotter's ideas about self-assessment, career development and change management (1978–1979); Stephen Covey's books on highly effective people (starting 1989); Marcus Buckingham's suggestions about discovering one's strengths (2001); Charles Handy's image of the *Shamrock Organization* (2002), with a professional core (the first leaf), project teams consisting of externally hired specialists (the second leaf) and a temporary workforce for production purposes (the third leaf); and Alfred Luthans' ideas about the psychological capital of organizations (2007). Just to name a few.[11]

This is not the book to get into all these theories, although the interested reader is cordially invited to take a closer look at them in further reading. It is important to note, however, that they have two things in common: i) all are basically optimistic in nature and ii) they all rest on the premise that individuals, organizations and maybe even society as a whole have developmental potential. One can easily see a direct line between Julian Rotter's strong internal locus of control and TMC's mantra of "You are in the driver's seat," your career and life are your YOUrney.

In a 2016 Pontes bureau presentation, Freek van Bedaf puts it this way: human talents are genetically predisposed, they are inborn. To unlock them requires energy and attention, attitude and focus. But if these forces are mobilized, even limited talents can be developed to some degree.

▌ THE CONSTRUCTION

Once Van Bedaf had defined the core of employeneurship, he wanted to detail the concept and find a way to measure it. This became a team effort. He formed a circle of top-level psychometrics and advisors, including: test maker Dr. Lolle Schakel; Pieter van Hoogstraten, a former general manager of PI Company, which specializes in assessment tools; psychologist and test maker Jim de Rooij, who co-owns an assessment agency (Slim); Dr. Nico Smid, a personality assessment expert and teacher at Groningen University; and Prof. Dr. Ir. Mathieu Weggeman, who teaches innovation management at Eindhoven University of Technology and also works as a consultant.[12]

Based on discussions with this circle of experts and on his earlier reading, Van Bedaf identified eleven types of behavior — or competences, as he calls them — and twenty-one work values that can be associated with employeneurship. As you can see, there are many cross-connections. Some of the labels even double as both a competence and work value.

EMPLOYENEURSHIP COMPETENCES AND ASSOCIATED WORK VALUES

Anticipation openness to change, resilience, self-management

Autonomy openness to adventure, authenticity, decisiveness (vigor), independence, self-confidence (self-reliance)

Connection openness to adventure, openness to co-operation, sociability, tact, trust (confidence)

Focus concentration, orderliness, performance, self-confidence (self-reliance), self-management, structure

Positivism optimism, resilience, self-management, sociability, trust (confidence)

Proactivity openness to adventure, decisiveness (vigor), expression (expressing oneself), performance, self-confidence (self-reliance), sociability

Responsibility decisiveness (vigor), independence, optimism, resilience, self-confidence (self-reliance), self-management

Self-interest performance, recognition, self-development, self-management

Self-management decisiveness (vigor), diligence, orderliness, performance, self-management, structure

Self-reflection decisiveness (vigor), self-confidence (self-reliance), self-development

Vigor (decisiveness) optimism, performance, self-confidence (self-reliance), self-development

In itself, this list was just a list, a table of elements. It would also be necessary to describe the relative importance these competences had for the employeneurship concept. To get to that point, Van Bedaf focused on the dynamics between a person's innate qualities, the outside world in which they move around, and the competences they develop during their journey through life. To visualize these dynamics, he connected the competences (and related work values) with two models:

- The 5Q model, outlined above, as a way to describe and arrange the full range of personal innate qualities
- The VUCA model, outlined in the introduction of this book, which describes today's social and professional world as volatile, uncertain, complex and ambiguous

When detailing the connection between the 5Qs and the competences, it became clear that there is considerable overlap. Most competences can be associated with more than one type of intelligence. Vigor, for example, is an element of both mental (IQ) and emotional (EQ) intelligence; autonomy of both mental (IQ) and spiritual intelligence (SQ). Proactivity belongs to emotional (EQ) and spiritual intelligence (SQ); and responsibility to both spiritual (SQ) and functional intelligence (FQ).

All in all, the competences illustrate that the Qs are not separate qualities. They are closely interconnected.

Multiple intelligence and competences

IQ (mental)	EQ (emotional)	SQ (spiritual)	FQ (fuctional)
autonomy	positivism	autonomy	anticipation
self-interest	self-reflection	self-interest	focus
vigor (decisiveness)	vigor (decisiveness)	self-reflection	self-management
	connection	responsibility	responsibility
	proactivity	proactivity	

Finally, Van Bedaf analyzed which Qs and competences would be best suited for optimal employeneurship in the VUCA world. This resulted in:

FOUR UNDERLYING DIMENSIONS OF EMPLOYENEURSHIP
Employeneurs…
a. Permanently look for the **progression** of their insights, self-awareness, knowledge and expertise.
b. Try to develop their **professional skills** to create value and success both for themselves and for the organization they are working for.
c. Are able to apply the competences resulting from that progression and development in a **dynamic context** (which means that they, when looking for a new project, have a high level of anticipation and seek effective connections with the outside world).
d. Distinguish themselves by **executional power**, the ability to realize goals. They know what they want and are focused on closing the gap between wanting and doing, intending and achieving.[13]

After this last step, the employeneurship construct was complete, context-related, dynamic and measurable.

SUMMARY
Seven Steps to the Employeneurship Construct:
1. Assemble theories of motivation and (social) learning
2. Choose models for describing personal qualities (the 5Q multiple intelligence model) and today's context (the VUCA model)
3. Formulate a general concept of employeneurship
4. Discuss and detail this concept with a circle of relevant experts
5. Formulate a list of relevant competences and work values
6. Describe the connection of the 5Qs and the competences
7. Analyze which Qs and competences are best suited for optimal employeneurship in the VUCA world

THE ASSESSMENT PROCEDURE

When talking about measuring employeneurship, one might wonder: what's the use? From Van Bedaf's point of view, the answer is simple. He's an optimist. As indicated earlier, he believes human qualities aren't fixed, stable, unchangeable. They can be developed. And this process of development should be approached as an active, conscious, cognitive process of social learning.

In simple words: people *can* change, to an extent, by their own effort, and with some help.

When I interviewed him in 2019, he used an analogy with tinnitus — an internal ringing in the ear, without any external sound. There is no clear-cut effective medical treatment for this. "The brain is flexible and has the ability to change its priorities" — again: to an extent. Yet, some people may benefit from psychotherapy which helps them to accept their condition and to learn to re-interpret the tinnitus as a harmless background noise. "The awareness that this ringing is a phantom sound, can diminish the distress," Van Bedaf said. Similarly, awareness of one's Qs, competences and work values can help individuals build on their strengths and work on their weaknesses.[14]

From that point of view, assessing one's level of employeneurship can be seen as an eye-opening moment.

According to Van Bedaf the assessment procedure he and his team of experts have developed mainly has a prognostic, functional purpose. It doesn't measure actual behavior but offers predictions. It basically provides an answer to two questions:[15]

- to what extent will this person be **capable** of behaving like an employeneur?
- which tools may be deployed to **develop** the person's behavioral patterns in a desired direction?

Generally speaking, a capability is determined by three factors:

- Talent (disposition, based on personality)
- Attitude (focus, orientation, based on values and choices)
- Skills (based on knowledge, experience and training)

The Pontes employeneurship assessment procedure uses a battery of existing tests to determine these three factors, plus a fourth factor, motivation.

Together, these four tests result in detailed scores for each of the eleven employeneurship competences and each of the twenty-one underlying work values. The scores are expressed in a percentage, ranging from 0 to 100.

If an employeneur is *skilled* in a specific competence, he or she is able to "show effective behavior in practice, in a situation that is applicable" to the competence. This will result in a score between 50 and 75 percent.

If an employeneur is *excellently skilled* in a specific competence, they are either highly talented in this area or highly motivated to develop this competence (or both). Such a high score may appear great, at

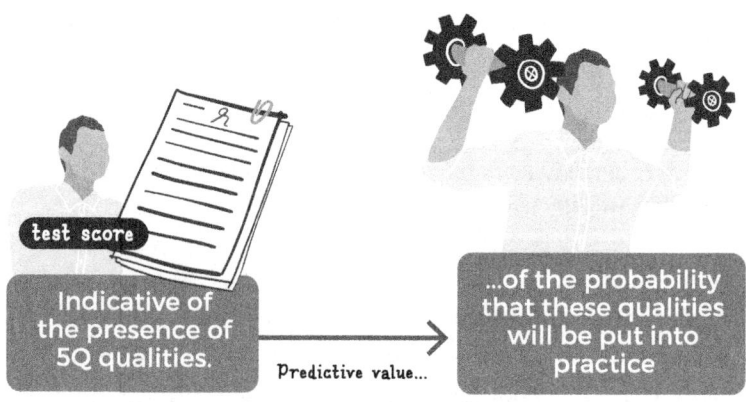

test score

Indicative of the presence of 5Q qualities.

Predictive value...

...of the probability that these qualities will be put into practice

first glance, but also implies a certain risk of imbalance. When a person focuses too much on developing one specific competence, they may neglect other competences.

If an employeneur is *unskilled* in a competence, they may have only a limited talent in this field, or lack motivation for its development (or both). In all cases, the competence requires extra attention.

Interestingly, this way of scoring shows that the highest score is not necessarily the best result. The most balanced employeneur will be someone with consistent scores at the skilled level.

MEASURING COMPETENCES (FOR DETAIL LOVERS)

Anticipation To what extent are you able, under pressure and in changing circumstances, to improvise, to maintain control or to decide to deliberately relinquish control?

Autonomy To what extent do you assume an attitude of independence; do you trust your own judgment; and do you claim the necessary space to determine your own direction and goals?

Connection To what extent do you focus on collaborating with others, on trusting them and on trying to understand them?

Focus To what extent do you work in a concentrated and targeted way towards your goal(s), without allowing yourself to be distracted?

Positivism To what extent do you expect things to develop in a positive way, and are you confident that you can find ways that will contribute to reaching your goals?

Proactivity To what extent do you take the initiative to come into action, to approach others and to address and solve problems?

Responsibility To what extent are you driven by a strong internal will and the conviction that you can influence your own success, and do you dedicate yourself to reaching your goals?

Self-interest To what extent do you want to be successful, do you want your successes to be recognized, and do you want to increase your market value?

Self-management To what extent do you not only show the will to achieve your goals but take concrete action, set priorities and show perseverance, even under pressure or in difficult circumstances?

Self-reflection To what extent do you reflect upon your role in certain situations, and upon the reasons for and consequences of your own behavior?

Vigor (decisiveness) To what extent do you analyze your successful experiences to be able to use your and other's strengths and weaknesses?

MEASURING WORK VALUES (FOR DETAIL LOVERS)

Adventure How important is it for you to work on projects that are new for you and that involve risk, uncertainty and possible surprises?

Authenticity How important is it for you to do work that you can fully support and that fits you as a person, without misrepresenting yourself?

Change To what extent are you open to change and experiment in your work?

Concentration To what extent do you keep your attention focused on the job or subject at hand and are you able to avoid distraction?

Co-operation How important is it for you to collaborate with others and to contribute to a good atmosphere and good mutual relations?

Decisiveness (vigor) To what extent will you come into action on your own initiative to handle matters or solve problems, instead of waiting until others (ask you to) do something?

Diligence To what extent do you dedicate yourself to do your work well, on time and as agreed, and will you do more than is expected?

Expression To what extent do you take the floor in a group meeting, do you approach others and do you feel at ease when being the center of attention?

Independence How important is it for you to determine your own goals and approaches, and to make your own decisions?

Optimism To what extent do you primarily see opportunities and do you primarily expect positive outcomes?

Orderliness To what extent do you work in a precise way and with an eye for detail?

Performance How important is it for you to deliver recognizable achievements, to experience success and to reach ever higher goals?

Recognition To what extent do you make it known which results you have achieved, and do you make sure these are recognized?

Resilience To what extent can you deal with adversity and criticism in a calm and moderate way, and are you able to put those negative aspects out of your head?

Self-confidence (self-reliance) To what extent are you confident in your work and in your ability to solve problems and handle situations?

Self-development How important is it for you to do work that offers you the opportunity to learn new things and to develop your knowledge and skills?

Self-management To what extent are you convinced that you can influence things and that your achievements depend on your dedication and not on sheer luck?

Sociability To what extent do you enjoy contact with others, having conversations and meeting new people?

Structure To what extent do you act in a planned and far-sighted way, and will you gather information and determine an approach before you get started?

Tact To what extent do you weigh your words, and do you consider other people's sensitivities and reactions before saying something?

Trust (confidence) Do you easily trust other people, and do you assume that their intentions are good, without them having to prove that first?

THE REALITY CHECK

What you have read so far about measuring competences, skill levels and work values, is theory. To be sure, the actual tests Van Bedaf and his team had selected, were validated. But their combination and usage in an employeneur assessment were not. To get some idea of what the assessment procedure would show in practice, they applied it to a hundred and fifty test subjects in three organizations — the idea being that the outcomes should reflect different employeneurship profiles per organization.

And they did.[16]

The comparison

The three organizations were TMC, the Dutch Metrology Institute (VSL) and Reinaerde, a care institution for people with limited abilities. The assessments took place in 2014–2015. As was expected, the average scores of their employees varied considerably.

At **TMC**, then with a staff of about 650, the employees had the highest total scores, and specifically high scores on autonomy, proactivity, self-interest and vigor (decisiveness).

At the **Dutch Metrology Institute**, with a staff of 150, scores were high on IQ but more average on other Qs. The employees scored highest on connection, responsibility and vigor (decisiveness) but relatively low on autonomy, self-interest and self-management.

At **Reinaerde**, an big care institution with a staff of 3,000, the average employeneurship score was low but with huge differences between individuals. In particular the Reinaerde staff showed a clear division between left-brainers (with high scores on mental intelligence [IQ] and spiritual intelligence [SQ]) and right-brainers (with high scores on emotional intelligence [EQ] and functional intelligence [FQ]).

The results also allowed for a comparison of the organizations' cultures. TMC had a demanding culture with high levels of pride and accountability, an emphasis on both connection and self-interest, and a lot of stress on autonomy, resilience, self-development and vigor (decisiveness). The Metrology Institute and Reinaerde were more bureaucratic, non-confrontational (but rather consultation oriented) and hierarchical.

Van Bedaf also compared scores at ASML and TMC and concluded that these were similar cultures but with one major difference: TMC favored visionary, thought leadership while the ASML culture was more IQ and alpha-male oriented.

The "ideal" employeneur and the "ideal" employeneurship culture

A few years and "a couple of thousand" more assessments later, Van Bedaf felt he had gathered enough impressions to sketch a tentative outline of the "ideal" employeneur — albeit without claiming any well-researched scientific basis. In his view:
- *balanced scores* on all Qs — the two on the left of the brain and the two on the right — clearly favor a successful development as an employeneur. Moreover,

- the single most important competence seemed to be *autonomy*, and
- the five most important work values seemed to be
  - *authenticity*
  - *independence*
  - *resilience*
  - *self-development* and
  - *vigor (decisiveness)*.

Balance between Qs can be improved, but low scores on autonomy and the five core work values would make it difficult to become a successful employeneur, he concluded. "These five are prerequisites, a *conditiones sine quibus non*," he wrote.

There's also something like an "ideal" employeneurship culture, a corporate culture that — in his view — offers the best circumstances for employeneurs to flourish. Not surprisingly, this ideal culture bears much resemblance to the TMC culture. It should be commercially ambitious, demanding, set high and clear goals and standards, offer much individual space, hold people accountable, focus on collaboration (but project based, not function based). It should also have a visionary leader, who has both hard and soft skills and shows modesty in claiming successes.

As the interviews in this book make clear, TMC does indeed deploy a wide array of tools to help its incoming, often rather left-brain, techies to develop both their hard *and* soft skills, to discover their strengths and weaknesses, and to find balance in both their personal life and their working life. Time and time again, the employeneurs refer to the important role played by their coaches, who might be described as their pilots, helping them to find their way through the changing tides, the treacherous currents, the hidden sandbanks and the looming storms. So let's, at the end of this chapter, meet one of those pilots.

AN INTERVIEW WITH ANETTE WIJNANDS, COACH

Anette Wijnands is head of coaching at Pontes Group. She was trained as a nurse and later became a full-time coach. She has been Freek van Bedaf's partner for twenty-five years and was intimately involved in the development of the employeneurship concept and assessment. The interview with her took place in late 2019 at the Pontes Group headquarters, in a stately mansion in the Dutch city of Breda.[17]

When TMC started, and Pontes still was part of the company, as TMC Assessment and Development, she had fourteen employeneurs to coach, she remembers. Less than a day's work. Today, forty Pontes coaches are coaching each — on average — twenty TMC employeneurs. "That will take them a day per week." What do they do on the other days? Well, Pontes has other clients too and, since the coaches work as freelancers, they have their own practice as well. Women are in the majority. The Pontes coaches vary widely in age: the youngest is 27, the eldest 60.

In the beginning, Anette says, the employeneurship concept was still very general in nature. "It was about leadership, about being pro-active. We already had a test in the beginning, but since then, we have developed that much further. Today's assessment is based on the five intelligences and is in fact part of a program of professionalization, which includes a special training of the coaches, who must be able to interpret the results."

Many people may have heard of IQ and EQ. But FQ and SQ are not so familiar.
"At first we described FQ as physical intelligence, but we have come to the point that we prefer functional intelligence. On the one hand, this concerns vitality, work/life balance but it also has to do with being able to organize that balance. So the F is broader than we thought. As for SQ, spiritual intelligence, that is about passion and motivation... maybe you have heard of the concept of ikigai [Japanese for a reason for being]? In essence that is about the question: for

what reason will you get out of bed in the morning? What makes you really happy?

"What we have found, and this is scientifically confirmed, is that if you coach and facilitate people to get access to all Qs, they will be more successful and happier. Those two are basically on one line."

In terms of coaching, making people aware of the role their Qs play may start with talking about obstructions, so about situations or experiences they find difficult to deal with, Anette says.

"Young professionals at highly dynamic companies such as ASML often want to talk about things they run into — their limits, in many cases. They will sigh, for example: I'm in four or five projects, so much is being asked of me! Then we will start talking about time management, and ask them: what is important to you, in what aspect do you want to develop yourself?"

TMC employeneurs tell us that much of the coaching is about personal matters.
"It's a holistic thing. A human being is holistic. If you have personal problems or are out of balance, that will express itself in your work. What also matters is the phase you're in. Juniors are facing other issues than seniors. All in all, the coaching is both work related and life related."

And what does TMC ask from you as coaches? Are you free to do what you want? Or do they ask you to coach their people towards becoming a successful employeneur?
"The goal is to develop people's employeneurship based on the behavioral patterns from the assessment. They do the assessment, after they have been hired, and discuss the results with their coach. Then the coach and employeneur will make a coaching agenda, which they will discuss with the cell director. So there's a direct link between the results from the assessment and the coaching agenda."

So it's all about: are you a good one for TMC, will you deliver the goods?
"Yes but at the same time it's about: do you want to develop yourself? Do you want to learn, pull yourself to a higher level? People who don't

want that will stagnate and become less flexible. TMC prefers people who are open to development and growth."

How important is the coach in all this?
"Important. We select them and train them so they are able to coach on the five Qs. They have to be familiar with the employeneurship concept, the assessment procedure and the TMC organization. To get there, they go through a process of accreditation. Only then can they start as a coach for TMC's employeneurs."

Anette explains that Pontes organizes its TMC-accredited coaches in coaching pools. Each of these pools has a specific specialization. "We have a pool with coaches who are strong in leadership coaching. Others are strong in time management coaching or in project management coaching. Some have worked at ASML or Philips themselves and are specifically familiar with those cultures. Of course, over time, a person's coaching need may change in character. In that case we will find him or her another coach."

Coaching itself has changed in character too, she adds. "In the past, the tendency was that we became involved when a conflict was looming or a burnout. Now we can often prevent that. If you coach someone on his/her Qs, you help them move in the right direction, take care of themselves and deal with difficult situations before things get out of hand. This reflects itself in TMC's low absenteeism."

Being healthy, she says, also means "Making sure that you're physically fit, being in connection with what you need, knowing what makes you happy." She returns to the ikigai concept and shows a picture of four overlapping circles, each containing three ikigai elements — or maybe: interpretations of what may be meaningful for a particular person — and together reflecting eight such interpretations:

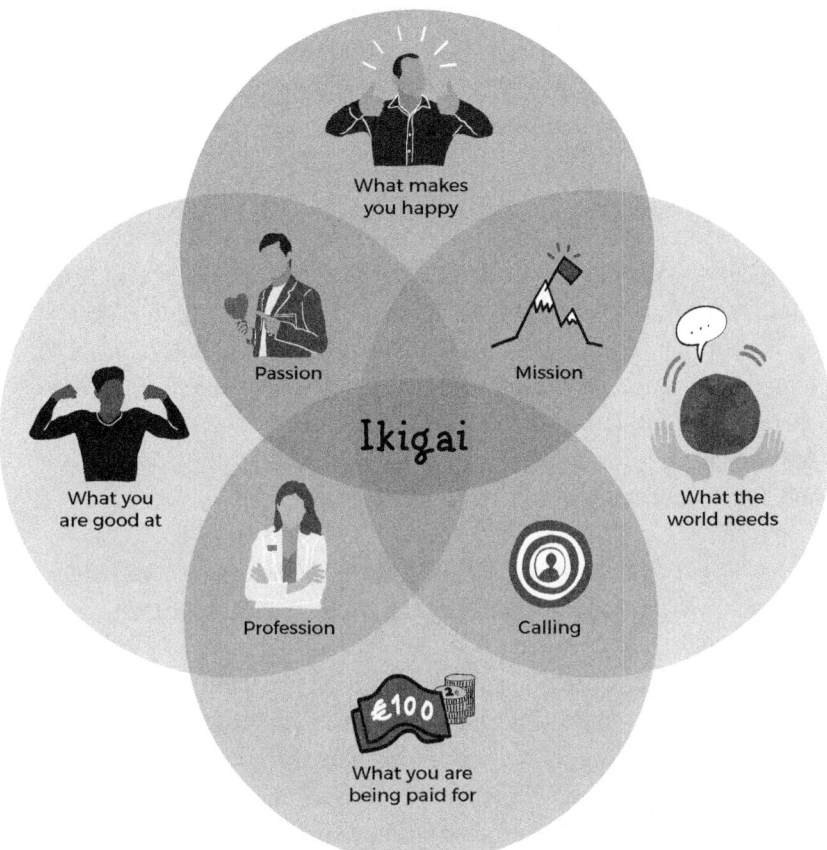

Passion

Mission

Ikigai

What you
are good at

What makes
you happy

What the
world needs

Profession

Calling

What you are
being paid for

"We see this as a model for developing 'personal leadership'," she adds. "Coaching means talking about these things, analyzing effective and less effective behavioral patterns, trying to find out what makes the person unhappy and what makes them positively happy."

But what if the coaching doesn't work? Surely that will happen too?
"Sometimes a person is not in the right role or in the right job. In case of such a mismatch, it will be necessary to look for alternatives. TMC is very flexible, they will go to great lengths to find another client for you. What's also important to realize: often, the potential for change within an existing job is bigger than expected. The coach can help you discover that potential, and help you distinguish between things you can and things you cannot change. We have many coaching processes in which people find out that their actual influence on

a difficult situation is greater than they think. Often it's a matter of communication, letting your boss or other people at your work know what you would want to see changed. That doesn't mean you're going to get it, but it may help. We do a lot of coaching on communication skills and styles."

"On the other hand, sometimes situations require acceptance to cope better. I often tell people: suppose you end up in prison as an innocent convict, for five years. You can choose one of two ways to deal with that: as a sufferer (in Dutch: *lijder*) or as a leader (in Dutch: *leider*, pronounced the same as *lijder*). You can continue feeling like a victim and complaining about the bad food, or you can start looking for a meaningful way to pass the time: take up a study, find a prison job, work out regularly to stay fit, et cetera."

As for the balance between work and private life. What struck me in the interviews with TMC employeneurs, is that this is a common theme. They all talk about that.
"That really is a contemporary thing. Young people in particular consider that as important. Once upon a time making a career was extremely important, now they want a more balanced life. Young fathers want 'daddy days'; others want to work from home at least one day per week. Not all organizations have the same flexibility in accommodating those wishes but we have spotted some frontrunners with a chief happiness officer."

Really? An executive who is responsible for employee well-being and happiness?
"Yes. That is still very exceptional, but I think there are a few even in the Netherlands."

CHAPTER 5

GOING ABROAD

"A REAL INNOVATION"

In April 2013, Emmanuel Mottrie left Altran. He had worked at the French high-tech and R&D consultancy firm since 1996. During those seventeen years, he had made quite a career. A Belgian national, he had studied business engineering in Leuven, international comparative management in Brussels and Japan, and philosophy at the Catholic University of Leuven. Before being hired by Altran, he had worked a few years in the marketing and sales department of Mazda Europe. Altran had given him in-company training and placed him in Belgium, where he helped expand the Belgian subsidiary. In 2001, he was promoted to CEO of De Valck Engineering, a secondment agency for drafting technicians that Altran had just acquired, and asked to integrate it into Altran group — which he did, successfully. In 2009, he was promoted again, this time to a member of the Altran board and CEO of Altran Benelux, with the assignment to first integrate the Altran businesses in Belgium and Luxemburg and then integrate those with the Dutch Altran business.[1]

In 2011, Altran asked Mottrie to also take charge of its subsidiary in the Netherlands, which had been operating at a loss since the 2009 worldwide financial crisis. It was around this time that he met Thijs Manders, whom Altran had approached with a takeover offer. Mottrie took part in the talks surrounding that offer as a board member and because he would logically be involved with a merger of TMC and the Dutch Altran branch.

The takeover did not work out, as we already know. Then, in 2013, Mottrie (who had become dissatisfied with certain company policies) and Altran went their separate ways. Mottrie decided to start his own consultancy. Just a few months later, in the summer of 2013, Thijs Manders contacted him. "I accepted out of courtesy," he remembered when I interviewed him in early 2019. "We had dinner, and I must say, first and foremost, I met some very sympathetic people: Thijs himself, Jan van Rijt, Rogier van Beek. Secondly, it turned out that we had exactly the same ideas about what high-tech and R&D consultancies should be like, the same values, which they had incorporated into a unique model, the employeneurship model. I considered that a real innovation for our sector. It was a model that I had never seen before. It was a people-driven model, and it was exactly for that reason it could be disruptive in an existing market, like a red spot in a blue ocean."[2]

Thijs Manders asked him to become the CEO of TMC Netherlands but during the follow-up talks, the two of them decided that Mottrie would set up TMC's first foreign branch, in Belgium, and expand it to around two-hundred employeneurs in five years' time. There were multiple reasons for such an expansion, Mottrie explained. "Being an international company makes us more interesting for potential employeneurs who want to pursue an international career. It will also make it easier for us to attract specialists from other parts of the world, and in these times of super-specializations we have to do that. Third: an increasing number of clients are international companies themselves. They asked us if we could send our specialists to their foreign subsidiaries too. If you want to be on their preferred supplier list, you have to be able to do that, wherever they need them." Finally, as Thijs Manders summarized during our January 2020 interview: "I saw that we couldn't become much bigger in the Netherlands."[3]

Stringing beads

On December 10, 2013, Mottrie signed a management contract with TMC, and in the spring of that year TMC Belgium was founded. The intended international expansion followed at a steady pace. In 2015, the group opened offices in France (first Rennes, in the west of the country, then Paris); in 2016 in Italy and Spain; in 2017 in Dubai; in 2018 in Sweden and Canada, in Portugal (Porto) and additional offices in three other French regions. After five years, the number of offices abroad had grown to eighteen in a total of nine countries. All of these had started as greenfield operations, so without acquisitions. "We didn't buy companies, we bought teams," Mottrie said. "Why? This is a disruptive model, a market challenger. You can't buy an existing company and expect them to play that role." In Belgium, he originally considered buying a small consultancy of — say — forty to fifty people and then expand it to two hundred but eventually he abandoned that idea. "That would have cost us €10 million. Now we invested between €1 million and €1.5 million and reached our goal faster." All the other new offices were set up in a similar way, he said, and with a similar investment. It was like stringing beads.[4]

The TMC Footprint for opening International Offices

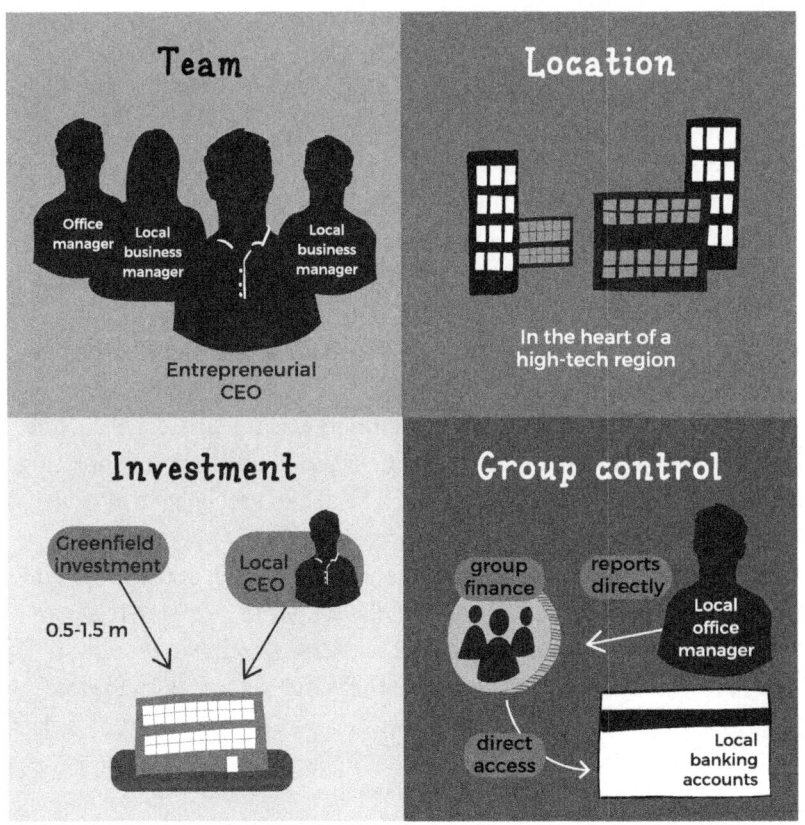

In Mottrie's view, a large part of the success of a new international TMC office depends on the CEO. "We want entrepreneurs, not managers. They have to have an entrepreneurial track record and have shown that they are able to build and expand something. They have to develop their own business plan and join as co-investor." Plus: "They have to share our values, because if you share the values, you don't need rules." Very important in Mottrie's eyes is that the CEOs of international offices truly understand the employeneurship concept. "This implies a totally different work relationship with your employees. Of course they are on our payroll, but we don't see them as employees, that is a 20th century thing. The point is: if you treat employees like children, they will behave like children. Treat them as employeneurs and they will behave like employeneurs. Our local CEOs must be able to allow their employeneurs autonomy, give them responsibility and stimulate their entrepreneurial attitude." Moreover, TMCs new international offices apply the five-pillar model right from the start, including the financial profit sharing, the transparency, the quarterly meetings, the employeneurship assessment, the coaching (the CEOs find local coaches, who are trained by Pontes), the training budget: the whole package.

At the time of this interview, February 2019, his first five years at TMC had almost passed. The Belgian target of two hundred was within reach (the actual number was 180). In 2018, TMC Belgium's revenue was €15.3 million, the net profit €2.7 million (which was a 17 percent EBIT). The Paris office had grown to one hundred employeneurs, the Italian one to fifty, the Spanish one to forty, the one in Sweden to around twenty-five, the rest were still small. The only office having trouble to get off the ground was the one in Dubai, due to the private circumstances of the CEO and the difficulty of opening a bank account in the emirate, which is an extremely lengthy and bureaucratic procedure. Around thirty percent of TMC's employeneurs were now working from international offices, and 23 percent of revenues were generated there. Thijs Manders' decision to seek further growth primarily across the borders, which had brought him to join forces with Gilde Buy Out Partners in 2012 and with Emmanuel Mottrie in 2014, had worked out.[5]

THE BELGIAN EXPERIENCE

Jaskaran Sandhu (TMC Belgium)[6]

If anyone can represent TMC's multinational footprint, it is Jaskaran Sandhu. He was born in India in 1985, moved to Europe with his parents when he was ten, studied in various European countries and worked in France, the Netherlands and Belgium.

His main study was aerospace engineering at Delft University of Technology, the Netherlands. After that, he worked for a while at Airbus Defence and Space in the Netherlands (formerly known as Dutch Space). Then, he moved on to TNO, initially working on space projects, then on a confidential ASML project. When I interviewed him in November 2019, he remembered, "At that point, in 2010, the French consulting company Altran approached me for leading a small team at ASML." He accepted. Then, a couple of years later, "I had the choice to join ASML permanently or stay at Altran." As a counteroffer, his business manager at Altran suggested that instead of converting to ASML he could set up his own business unit within Altran. With good reason. During his secondment at ASML the number of Altran consultants at that company had grown from five to over fifty. "A big part of that expansion came from the activities I was doing there." It was an attractive offer. His new business unit — which would ulti-mately be under the supervision of Emmanuel Mottrie, who had been put in charge of the Altran activities in both Belgium and the Neth-erlands — would be responsible for all Altran consultancy projects at ASML but also at other high-tech companies in the region, such as Philips Electronics and NXP. So Jaskaran accepted.

As mentioned earlier, Emmanuel Mottrie left Altran in 2013 and joined TMC in early 2014. After taking Matthias Warlop and Nassim Daoudi on board, he contacted Jaskaran. Exactly at the right mo-ment, it turned out. Despite being able to run his own business unit, he was losing interest in the secondment business. "I had worked in it as a consultant and as a manager. It was an industry with too many secrets and not transparent enough." As far as he was con-cerned, TMC was just another face in that industry. He had met TMC employeneurs at ASML, "But these guys weren't very open about what was so special about TMC." All he knew was, "That they were happy with TMC and that it was difficult to lure people away from TMC." But when he talked with Emmanuel Mottrie and Thijs Manders it soon became clear to him that their company was indeed quite different from Altran. And when he subsequently visited the TMC offices — then still at the Flight Forum — and met other TMC people, he was won over completely. "What I saw was a group of people who were really working together. In Altran, you were working solely for yourself and your own success. Plus, I saw a group that was always putting the consultant at the center." Altran made him a counteroffer that was (financially) far higher than he would get at TMC — which he regarded more or less as an insult, because if they considered him worth more, why hadn't they paid that before?

So he made his decision. "I had told my friends at Altran that I would never work at a consultancy again but now I decided to help Emmanuel with setting up the activities in Belgium." What had made the difference? On the one hand dissatisfaction with his employer. "I was almost at the point that I wanted to leave Altran. I had certain disagreements concerning the strategy and vision of the company. In order to grow, they had acquired two companies, but I felt these did not fit in the setup." On the other hand were "the openness, the transparency, the positive atmosphere at TMC" which he found "very attractive." On top of that came "the possibility to help build something from scratch, in accordance with my own vision." He moved to TMC in August 2014, a few months after Emmanuel, Matthias and Nassim.

What did you think of the word 'employeneur'? You still seem to use the word 'consultant' instead of 'employeneur' quite often...
He laughs. "It's something that — eh — takes time to get used to. But once you understand the mindset behind it, that is the least of the hurdles. And you know: it's a word that attracts attention and makes people think. When I talk to our clients, I always talk about 'our employeneurs', and it sticks in their mind. It's the surprise factor of the word, it makes them think. And then they try to use it themselves and they also start remembering it." He laughs again.

Building a business

So what was building TMC Belgium like? Emmanuel Mottrie started the new office with two directors (Mathias Warlop and Nassim Daoudi) and one business manager: Jaskaran. Within a year Mottrie promoted Jaskaran to director and partner. During the first years the team "wasn't just building a business but also building an environment," Jaskaran said. "Which meant starting an Entrepreneurial Lab, coaching, a YOUniversity, et cetera."

Let's first look at the business building part. You weren't familiar with the Belgian market. How did you find clients?
"We focused on a niche market, on something that nobody else was offering. One of our first contacts was actually with IMEC, in the city of Leuven. This is the largest research center in Belgium, the Belgian equivalent of TNO, you might say, but much closer to the industry. IMEC is very important. Many developments at Apple, at Google, at ASML could not take place without IMEC. It is very important in nanoelectronics and all kinds of state-of-the-art technologies. Today at any given time we have around twenty-five employeneurs at IMEC, which, by the way, is also our biggest client."

How did you convince them to hire your TMC employeneurs?
"We knew that IMEC was investing in the advanced [silicon wafer] patterning center, together with ASML and several other lithography companies. At the time there were two hundred TMC employeneurs working at ASML. IMEC didn't yet work with outside consultants, but we went to them and said: you are building an advanced patterning center, you can't get the guys you need for it but we have them. And by the way, if we're not mistaken you are building this center together with ASML, who already is our biggest client."

That made an impression. To prove that it could really deliver, TMC Belgium immediately presented the team it would bring along, consisting of some team members from Jaskaran's ASML period who had joined him in his transfer to TMC.

It was a significant breakthrough for young TMC Belgium. "Gaining IMEC as a client was great for our reputation." Building on that reputation helped the Belgian branch to acquire other important clients such as TREMEC, a producer of transmission systems for high-performance sports cars and heavy duty vehicles, which is located near Bruges; Punch Powertrain, another manufacturer of automotive transmissions and powertrains; and the engineering branch of ELIA Group, a Belgian high-voltage electricity transmission operator.

Building a reputable client base also helped to attract new employeneurs. The Belgian TMC team manages to find them all over the world, Jaskaran said. "A little less than half are Belgian, a quarter have other European nationalities, the rest are non-European," he estimated. There's only one criterion: "We look for the best engineers; we don't care where they come from."

The TMC model is Dutch in origin. Does it suit people from other countries and other continents?
"Our clients and our candidates usually have never heard of the TMC model. So you need to educate them. Some cultures are more open to the model than others. Candidates from India, for example, are very excited to hear about the financial transparency. We have a lot of consultancies in India, big volumes, but it's definitely not transparent there. With people from North Africa, like Tunisia, it's a bit more challenging to explain the profit share, because for them, the certainty of a high fixed salary is very important. Belgium on the other hand has a tax structure in which taxes rise very quickly; so when we talk with Belgian candidates we focus less on the fixed salary itself but more on the overall package and benefits."

Building a community

Founding a Belgian subsidiary also meant implementing all five pillars of the TMC model and building a Belgian TMC community, with business cells, pizza sessions, an Entrepreneurial Lab, et cetera.

Of course, the number of employeneurs was still small at the outset, so it wasn't yet useful to organize them in cells, Jaskaran explained.

"Given that the cells are ideally forty to eighty people, we now have three cells. So obviously we have more competences in one cell, we have groups of competences. In my group we have six, with software, electronics and IT as the general ones and physics, nanotechnology and data technology as the niche ones."

The only thing TMC Belgium does not have, Jaskaran said, are the competence groups within cells. And as for the pizza sessions, "We don't call them that here. We call them impact sessions." Why? "Because we don't have pizza." He laughs. "We have better food."

According to Jaskaran, TMC Belgium is even taking these sessions one step further. In his vision, "We have the best engineers, and what we need to do is show ourselves as an expertise center, not just as a company that is providing consultants. TMC should be seen as the company you need to go to if you need specific expertise. So we do not only have internal sessions, but also do sessions with the clients, so basically conferences. We organized our first conference last month and there were more than eighty people, with many of our major clients." This specific conference was about an innovative way of developing software. "TMC has become a development partner in a research company that is developing software in a specific way. We are not a financial partner but we invest in training. For this conference we invited our clients in the software domain so they could talk with the professor who is responsible for this specific development method."

How about the international TMC community? How are the contacts between the international offices?
"That is something TMC has done very well. We all know each other. Every six months or so we organize the TMC Fundamentals meeting [one of which was described earlier in the book] where every new manager or director, no matter in which country, should come to this three-day program in Eindhoven. That way you get to know your colleagues, learn about the TMC way of working, and you can exchange ideas and best practices."

But today, the international organization is still relatively small. How will these contacts develop if TMC expands?

"As the individual country offices grow, what can indeed happen is that they turn their focus inwards. In itself that is not an issue, as long as we keep in mind that together as one company we are stronger than divided over the — say — ten countries that we are in today. Today our strength is that each country brings in its way of working and its competences. So, for example, Spain is focusing on digitalization, so I know if we also want to do something in that domain, we should use that expertise. The same if other countries want to do something in nanotechnology: they should know that TMC Belgium is very strong in that area."

Will this not result in competition between the various offices when they are looking for engineers with very specific expertise?

"That is why we reward every partner for collaboration. So if we need to help a certain customer in Belgium and a colleague in France or the Netherlands sends me a candidate for that customer, there is a reward for that. There is a profit sharing element in that [the TMC Square program]."

TMC stimulates interactions between the international offices in other ways too. There are weekly calls, the CEOs have their own WhatsApp group and they meet four times per year. In a follow-up interview in September 2020, group CEO Emmanuel Mottrie gave an example of where this exchange of ideas can lead to. "In Belgium, we set up a young graduates program. Via the student associations, we collect resumes of 1,300 engineering graduates. We invite 130 of them, assess them in groups of twelve and offer the best two of each group a contract. This program has become one of the factors behind our strong position in the Belgian market, and we are now introducing it in other countries too."[7]

THE FRENCH EXPERIENCE

Loïc le Mené (TMC Paris)[8]

When I asked Jaskaran Sandhu whether he had any French employeneurs working for him in Belgium, he answered affirmatively. According to him, French candidates usually enter their first meeting with TMC with an attitude of skepticism. "But by the time you have explained the model, they are much more open to talk. For them it is: they have seen the worst side of consultancy, that is, being used as commodity, not having any influence whatsoever on the company, not being as well paid as in Belgium, being thrown from one project to another."

One day later, Loïc le Mené, the CEO of TMC's office in Paris, confirms this picture. "At first I thought it was just another model in the consulting and secondment industry, but in the end I was attracted by the liberal aspect of the model."

Le Mené, who is forty, doesn't conceal the fact that initially, he was primarily attracted by the money TMC offered him to set up his own office. He was born in the north, "Between Lille and Paris, in the deep countryside of France, into the Belgian culture, which is more Anglo-Saxon than the French culture." He studied in Lille and Compiègne and started working for Safran, a huge manufacturer of aviation, aerospace and defense equipment, such as missile engines (for the Ariane missile), airplane and helicopter engines, landing gear, wiring systems and aviation electronics. After four years, he became an account manager at a small secondment agency, recruiting engineers and finding projects for them at customers. After another four years — in 2015 — he decided to start his own consultancy. "Then, by coincidence, I met Emmanuel Mottrie, who told me about the employeneurship model and the plans to launch TMC internationally." In fact, the meeting wasn't all that coincidental. TMC had just started its first French office, in the city of Rennes, and had hired one of Loïc's friends to help set that up. The friend then introduced him to Mottrie. "I was in the process of starting my own thing, but I was a bit weak financially. So I thought: OK, let's do it this way. I started in November 2015."[9]

The challenge: to find the right people

He hadn't chosen the easiest job. Within four years he would have to build an office of one hundred employeneurs, then grow to two hundred in the next four. Looking even further ahead, the potential for TMC Paris was estimated at five hundred. Finding projects in the huge Paris region wouldn't be the hardest part. But how to find the people? "It's a great challenge to find employeneurs in France," Loïc said. "Because you know, employeneurship is about self-determination and freedom. And in the French mindset, especially in the engineer's one, it is crucial to be secure. And that is what is difficult with the employeneurship over here, although it is easier with young engineers, who are somewhat more in the entrepreneurship mindset."

But even if the self-determinative aspect of the employeneurship concept doesn't immediately appeal to French engineers, pillar number three of the TMC model — the permanent contract and the long-term relationship — does. Loïc le Mené: "When TMC began offering permanent contracts in the Netherlands in 2000, it was probably disruptive because of the flexible contracts and temporary work you have over there. But in France everybody is working on a permanent contract and it is very difficult to break the employees from the companies. So in France, security is not disruptive; the security of the permanent contract is a must-have."

What is disruptive, is TMC's financial transparency towards its employees. "That is even more disruptive than the individual profit sharing. In France it is hard to talk about money. The other [secondment] companies are playing with that. They hire people at low cost and sell the service at higher cost. In between there is a black box they don't talk about. Even when I was a manager in another agency, I was not aware what was in the black box. So the transparency is breaking barriers more than the profit sharing."

As for the practical part of finding employeneurs: that was and is yet another challenge. "We have just one online job board for engineers, Apec, set up by an association of engineers. Otherwise, we don't have suitable job boards, and they are very expensive." On top of that: the market for engineers is very tight. Le Mené: "For many decades, the engineering job has been undervalued in France, in terms of salary and in terms of social recognition. So now, everybody wants to go to business school rather than to a technical university." Recruitment in France means networking, he explains. He found a considerable number of his engineers by approaching them via LinkedIn and luring them away from the industrial groups they were working for. Hiring directly from universities is not really effective, he said. Graduates from the *école polytechnique* and other *grandes écoles* — where France's future governmental and corporate elite is educated — will usually go straight to top jobs in the civil service, manufacturing and finance. The second tier technical universities also produce well-trained engineers, "But the customers want our candidates to have at least some years of experience," Loïc said. "It is good for us to do marketing towards these schools, so they know us, but not to hire their students directly after graduation."

Another reason for him not to hire graduates straight from university is that TMC Paris doesn't want to compete with major secondment agencies like Altran and Alten. They place a lot of young, relatively inexperienced people in the outer and middle layers of their clients' workforces, effectively providing extra hands (capacity). Remember the concentric circles Hans Strieder drew in chapter 1? TMC wants to second its people in the technological core of its clients. In line with that, Loïc le Mené said, "We are more into providing expertise, we also have young people, but only if they have the capability and maturity."[10]

"The war is to get the candidates, not to get the customers"

According to Le Mené, the shortage of engineers in France has resulted in a quite paradoxical situation. "If you have the best candidates you will get the customer. So the war is on getting the candidates, not on getting the customers. If you can find the engineers, then you are okay." It is by focusing on the best engineers that TMC Paris has been able to grow, he said. "That model gives us a substantial advantage."

So what kind of customers does TMC Paris serve? According to Loïc, they are in all kinds of sectors: the automotive industry (with big players like Renault) but also smaller companies in the medical devices industry and the defense industry, who don't require extra capacity but skills and expertise. Because of the "paradoxical situation" described earlier, TMC Paris doesn't have a specific sector approach towards acquiring clients. It's rather the other way around. The client has to offer the right conditions and project(s) to suit the employeneur in his further professional and personal development. Loïc le Mené: "Our employeneurs can go to the automotive sector, to defense, to a big customer, to the smallest one, we try everything. We are very open minded in terms of the skills we require, as long as it is engineering. The thing is, we expect our candidates to fit in the employeneurship model, in terms of value and mindset and personality. And we propose him to the customer from that point of view. Maybe it is not politically correct what I say, but the customer for us is not so important, the most important is: we need the customer to bring the engineering sector in France towards the employeneurship model. Other secondment companies use engineers as resources to serve the customer, we use the customer as resources to serve our employeneurs."

As arrogant as this may sound, TMC Paris did indeed see its number of employeneurs and its revenues grow steadily throughout 2016– 2019 to close to a hundred engineers and €8.5 million. One problem did emerge, though, precisely because of the labor market shortages. Loïc le Mené: "Last year, we lost ten candidates because Safran began hiring them." Like ASML did in the Netherlands, Safran demanded that seconded engineers convert to contracts at the company. According to Loïc, fifty percent of the TMC employeneurs seconded at Safran refused the conversion. Which he considered an excellent score: "At other consulting companies, 99 percent will accept."

Yet another problem was the increasing tension in trade relations between the USA and Europe and the USA and China. At the time of the interview, late 2019, the effects on the automotive industry in particular were becoming visible. Loïc remained optimistic, though. In his view, the trade tensions did have impact on sales and production but less so on research and development in the automotive industry. "We have some employeneurs in the production sector, working on quality and new product introduction. So we do feel a bit worried about the factory activity in the automotive sector, but not yet on the research and development. There are so many technological changes in the automotive sector, like the autonomous vehicle, the electric vehicle, artificial intelligence in the car, so there is still a lot of work in R&D. If they don't do R&D, they will die."

In general, the aerospace and defense industry in France is an interesting market for TMC France as well, and the company has several clients in this sector (Thales and Safran, in particular). To focus a little more on this sector, TMC opened an office in Toulouse — the home base of Airbus Industries. But according to Loïc le Mené, the aerospace industry is a rather closed market and — moreover — requires security clearances and special certification to work in.

THE SWEDISH EXPERIENCE

Åsa Åhlander (TMC Göteborg)[11]

Is the Dutch model transplantable to France, I asked Loïc le Mené, and he answered: "There are employeneurs all over the world, you just have to know your market and adapt the model. Not the basic structure, but in how you present it to the engineers and to the customer. You have to find the right pitch in the country's spirit. The transparency is important to French engineers and maybe some other aspects are important to Swedish engineers."

Which aspects? I asked Åsa Åhlander, the CEO of TMC Sweden, a week later. "The profit sharing and the coaching part are the biggest thing for employeneurs in Sweden. And I know transparency is very important as well." If we take the answers to this question from Jaskaran Sandhu, from Loïc le Mené and from the participants of the TMC Fundamentals sessions earlier in this book, the inevitable conclusion is that the TMC pillars appeal — one way or another, to varying degrees — to people from many cultures.

Åsa Åhlander is forty-five and was born in Lidköping, a town in the western part of Sweden. She studied economics and psychology, acquired an MBA, and has been working in the consulting/secondment business for fifteen years. Before she moved to TMC, she ran the high-tech and R&D consultancy department (with around five hundred engineers) of the Swedish branch of Experis, a recruitment agency and consultancy with offices in eighty countries.[12]

Exchanging a managerial job at a big company for a start-up sounds like quite a step. "I was born and bred in a big company and I needed a new perspective. They [Experis] were a good company with good people but did what they had always been doing. They were talking about the new generation that was coming into the market, and about teaching the clients how to adapt to that change and about what they needed to do to attract new talents, et cetera. But we didn't do these things ourselves. So there was a contradiction in what I said to my clients and my own beliefs." In brief: Experis wasn't innovative enough to her liking. "I had always been an 'intrapreneur' at Experis, always wanted to develop new things and also got the chance to prove them, but when I came across TMC in the summer of 2017 and heard about the employeneurship model, that really fit my beliefs."

She was just setting up a new project for Adecco Group in Sweden but decided to abandon it. "I had been implementing a new brand (Modis) for them. When TMC called me in July 2017, this project was just half a year old. So it was bad timing because Swedish people usually do what they have promised. But when I talked with Emmanuel Mottrie I was convinced that this was actually what the market needed but didn't know it yet. It took me a couple of weeks, but then I knew I had to go with my gut feeling, that this was a chance to establish this in Sweden. And I decided to go through the recruitment process and everything." The process took half a year. She talked with TMC people a couple of times and did some market research to assess the potential for a Swedish TMC branch. In December 2017, the contract was signed. In early 2018, two offices were launched, one in Skövde (a town in south Sweden) and one in Gothenburg, on the west coast.

A people development business

What really attracted her? "A lot of companies attract with external factors and motivations like money, and I don't believe in that.

Of course people should feel safe, secure and respected. Remember Maslov and his pyramid. But true motivation doesn't come from external driving forces. It comes from yourself, from within. And that's what I like about the model, as an employeneur you can choose what you would like to work on for a certain time. Now I would like to work in the lab and now I want to work on myself. It is up to me, I take my own responsibility in how I can develop myself."

Interestingly, Åhlander has the same market approach as Loïc le Mené in Paris. "We don't recruit in line with the needs of the customer, we recruit the people we want." In other words: we are not in the customer development business, we are in the people development business. And it works. "We recruit the people we want and during the recruitment process they give their wishes and thoughts about what kind of projects they would like to participate in and at which potential clients. This way of working has made us strong and also helped us to acquire many clients, we actually acquired fifty employeneurs and twenty-nine clients in eighteen months. That is really good, and I am glad about it. And that's what happens when you allow the employeneurs to take the driver's seat. I could say to them: I think you should work at Ericsson or another company. They have a perfect background for that, but then they don't take responsibility for their own career. So I give them responsibility, I fully trust them and I give them autonomy to do it the way they want."

One thing is certain, this approach selected a bunch of very motivated employeneurs. Just a few days before the interview, Åsa was confronted with two departures, two people who decided to transfer to another secondment agency because it offers them a higher salary. "That's just two in eighteen months," she said. "Well, I don't take up that (salary) battle." She could afford that attitude. The total number of employeneurs in Sweden at the time of the interview had reached the magic number of fifty, which was five above projection. To find them, Åsa employs a variety of methods. "Through our network, we use LinkedIn as a recruitment tool — which a lot of companies in Sweden do — and via referral. We get about forty percent of our people because they are referred to us by our current employeneurs."

When we talked at the end of 2019, TMC Sweden had one somewhat larger business cell — manufacturing support — and three fledgling cells: new product introduction, software and data science. As in other countries, all five pillars had been introduced right from the start and, yes, Åsa answered, there had been some pizza sessions, "But still mainly to meet each other, more office-oriented than business-oriented."

As in Belgium and France, TMC of course had to build itself a name and a reputation with new clients. Like Jaskaran Sandhu in Brussels and Loïc le Mené in Paris, Åsa had — and still has — to spend a lot of time explaining the five-pillar model. She found that many clients don't really understand it until "They see our people go away from their work to meet the coach and hear them talk about TMC and about employeneurship." Then they become curious. They also have to get used to the independent and self-confident attitude of TMC employeneurs. With a smile, Åsa said, "Of course, the purchasing department of the biggest companies may say: those people of yours will only be really good at negotiating and increase the sales price. But if I ask them to put themselves in the seat of the employeneur, then they like the concept. And who wouldn't?"

CHAPTER 6

THE CLIENT

"MY BEST MOVE EVER"

Meet Marijn van Os and his development company Innoluce. When I visited him in March 2019, the company was nine years old. Actually, he didn't own it anymore. He sold it in 2016 to Infineon, a German electronics firm that was spun off from Siemens, and has around forty thousand employees and turnover of more than €8 billion. Marijn's Innoluce is a spin-off too. For twelve years, he was employed by Philips Electronics. First he worked at Philips' Center for Industrial Technology (the renowned Centrum voor Fabricagetechnologie, CFT), then he built a Philips factory in the Czech Republic, and finally he returned to the CFT — which, meanwhile, had been renamed Philips Applied Technologies. Then, in 2010, Philips handed him the ownership of a series of patents for a laser application he had developed and he began his own company. "So far, my best move ever," he said.[1]

We were sitting in a meeting room in a nondescript, modern, two-story office building in an equally nondescript industrial area in the suburbs of Nijmegen, a medium-sized provincial town in the east of the Netherlands. On the table were two mugs with coffee, my notepad, my pencil, and a small (one inch) square piece of plastic with some electronic components and an extremely tiny mirror, resting on a set of even tinier leaf springs. Marijn explained that I was looking at a micro-electronic mechanical system (MEMS), a system that combines micro-mechanics with micro-electronics. In this case it's a miniature laser scanner. Infineon bought it because it is essential technology for adjusting the laser beams in high-performance light detection and ranging (lidar) systems. On its website, Infineon offers the following context: "Lidar, radar and camera will be the three key sensor technologies for semi-automated and fully automated cars. While radar uses radio-frequency electromagnetic waves, lidar employs laser beams to measure the distance to objects adjacent to the car. Scanning lidar systems help to detect small objects on the road."[2] "This is a very big development," Marijn said. "The range of applications is expanding fast." Innoluce's laser scanning modules are — for example — suitable for laser headlight systems. These are capable of increasing the driver's range of visibility at night to up to six hundred meters and allow the lighting beams to follow the curves of the road. The modules are also suitable for automatic "lane keeping" and "adaptive cruise control" systems, which help the driver to keep the car in the correct lane and allow for quick speed adaptations in case of sudden traffic jams. Further down the line, Innoluce's miniature laser scanning modules will also be key elements in "highway pilot" systems — a combination of lane keeping, adaptive cruise control and other navigation features that are elementary in the development of self-driving cars. All of these systems require the constant scanning of and feedback from the environment to help the vehicle adapt its movements.[3]

TMC has been a crucial support for Innoluce, in various ways, Marijn said. "I already worked with TMC experts in my Philips days, and when I started Innoluce, I immediately called them. In fact, we did all our development since 2010 with TMC people." At the outset, the co-operation was a bit uneasy. The first expert TMC sent over proved to be a mismatch and was quickly replaced. After that, things went better. The key, Marijn said, was TMC's flexibility. "When we had a quiet period and asked them to reduce the number of working days of their people to three for a while, they easily agreed. And when we ran into liquidity problems and had to do a financial restructuring, they agreed to a delayed payment." When Van Os offered Rogier van Beek, TMC's chief financial officer, a debt-equity conversion, Van Beek declined. "But all in all they thought along with us and were able to think like entrepreneurs."

At the time of the interview, Innoluce had a staff of about eighteen people, six of whom are TMC. Marijn knew all their names by heart: Ruben, Tommy, Maria, Alie, Christina and Michiel. He was aware of many of the TMC model's features: the long-term contract, the bonus system, the coaches (who visit the TMC employeneurs at the office). He had some discussions with TMC about conversion: like

ASML and other companies, Innoluce's mother Infineon sometimes wanted to transfer an external expert to its own payroll — which TMC didn't like of course. But his personal contact with TMC's account manager was good. And he definitely liked TMC's intellectual property policy: "technology developed by TMC experts will be transferred to us after two years, free of charge. That's better than TNO. Technology developed by their experts remains TNO's exclusive property for two years and after that you continue to pay a royalty."

The Market as seen by TMC

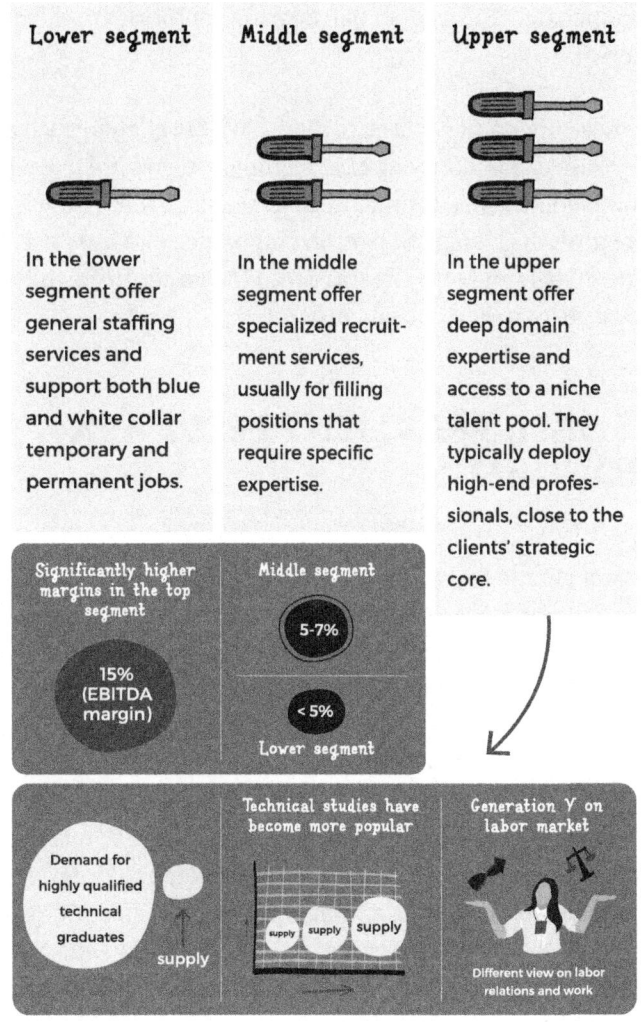

Lower segment

In the lower segment offer general staffing services and support both blue and white collar temporary and permanent jobs.

Middle segment

In the middle segment offer specialized recruitment services, usually for filling positions that require specific expertise.

Upper segment

In the upper segment offer deep domain expertise and access to a niche talent pool. They typically deploy high-end professionals, close to the clients' strategic core.

Significantly higher margins in the top segment

15% (EBITDA margin)

Middle segment

5-7%

< 5%

Lower segment

Demand for highly qualified technical graduates

supply

Technical studies have become more popular

supply supply supply

Generation Y on labor market

Different view on labor relations and work

Is Innoluce a typical TMC client? Yes and no. Maybe the best answer is: there is no typical TMC client. The clients do have similarities. Almost all of them are active in high-tech industries and spend a lot of energy (and time and money) on research and development. In its home market, the Netherlands, TMC can boast a blue chip client base featuring (subsidiaries of) companies like ASML, Bosch, DAF Trucks, Demcon, DSM, Johnson & Johnson, Merck, NXP, Océ, Philips Electronics, Royal Dutch Shell, TNO and Vanderlande Industries (a manufacturer of internal transport systems). Abroad too, the number of big, blue chip clients is growing, with names like Anheuser-Busch InBev (the biggest beer producer in the world), Airbus, Energie de France (EDF), research & development company IMEC, Punch Power Train, Siemens, SKF (Swedish Ball Bearing Factory), Total, Volvo Cars and others.[4]

Next to those big names there are many smaller clients, such as Innoluce. In France, a majority of TMC's employeneurs are placed at such small and medium-sized companies. As we shall see, TMC is focusing its future growth strategy in part on companies like Innoluce, which specialize in R&D and offer an entry into the larger firms in which they are or ultimately will be incorporated.

A SOBERING CLIENT FEEDBACK PROGRAM

What do our clients feel about us? Every company should of course be interested in that and to find out, many companies ask their clients to give them digital feedback — usually consisting of a simple rating system or possibly a short survey. Only few of them take the trouble TMC took in 2017 and 2018: to arrange a series of long interviews at four important client companies in the Netherlands: Bosch, DAF Trucks, TNO and Vanderlande Industries. It was a bold exercise, which demanded not just quite a bit of time from TMC but also from staff at the client companies. Yet, almost all potential interviewees consented, which resulted in a total of twenty-five meetings. When they were asked to express their overall opinion on a scale of zero to ten, they gave TMC an average of 7.9. That it wasn't an eight was caused by the lowest mark (a three), which was a bit of an anomaly, since all the other marks were seven or higher.[5]

A 7.9 might be considered a good score, but it is indicative of TMC that it applied a more severe standard, the Net Promoter Score, which serves as "an indicator of the loyalty and advocacy customers show for a company" and was developed by Fred Reichheld, a consultant at Bain & Company (USA) and author of *The Loyalty Effect* (1996) and *The Ultimate Question 2.0* (2011).[6]

The Net Promoter Score focuses on two categories of clients: the detractors (who score you at six or below) and the promoters (who score you at nine or ten). The passives are of no interest to customer loyalty. To get a positive NPS, the percentage of promoters has to surpass the percentage of detractors.

In the 2017–2018 client interviews TMC received Net Promoter Scores between zero and forty, and an average of twenty-four. Now a 7.9 out of 10 will probably make most people quite satisfied. But a score of twenty-four out of a hundred offers much less reason for complacency — which was probably the effect TMC wanted to bring about. The client feedback exercise should be a wake-up call and a learning experience.

So what were these four clients happy with? And with what less so? First of all, they had a lot of positive remarks about TMC's people and especially so about the employeneurs. These were highly qualified and professional, had good resumes, were well prepared for their initial interviews and well suited for the project they would be working on. The account managers, too, received positive remarks about their professionalism and accessibility, although some interviewees complained that they never seemed to stick around very long and didn't always notify them about their replacement.

As far as TMC's visibility as a company was concerned, two elements had drawn the clients' attention: i) the fact that it invested in its employeneurs and ii) the pizza sessions it organized with and for clients. The latter in fact tasted so good as to make them want more of it. That was positive, but at the same time that was about it. Three quarters of the interviewees indicated that they knew little about TMC's cells and specializations, and were in the dark about the company's strategy, its international activities, its gender policy and its view on corporate social responsibility. And even though the interviewees almost unanimously commended the quality of TMC's employeneurs, not all of them were aware that the group positioned itself in the top segment of the high-tech and R&D consultancy market. Some put the company on a par with competitors in that top segment but others with competitors in the middle and lower segments.

The feedback interviews revealed that clients would appreciate
- a more pronounced corporate image
- more active and frequent communication with TMC (not just with employeneurs and account managers but also at the management level and via newsletters, social media and events)
- a more outspoken and visible corporate strategy, which should include elements like market positioning, specialization, internationalization, corporate social responsibility and gender policy

- a more structural and strategic implementation of the service provider-client relationship

So maybe they — unwittingly — asked for a book like this (and some other things).

Now remember that this was late 2017, early 2018. TMC had been on the international road for just three years. Its operations in Belgium and France (Paris and Rennes) were doing well, on the whole, its international business was growing fast, but its offices in Sweden, southwest and south of France and North America hadn't yet been opened. Moreover, at the time of the feedback program, the company was in fact in the early stages of developing the new, comprehensive, ambitious and expansive strategy the clients were asking for.

STEPPING UP AMBITION

That strategy will be outlined in the next chapter. For now, I'd like to point to a shift in ambition which became visible in 2018, no doubt as a result of that strategic exercise and possibly also as a result of the positive, yet sobering 2017–2018 client feedback. I stumbled on that shift when comparing TMC's mission statements of 2011 and 2018. Take a look.

- In 2011, TMC wrote in its mission statement: "we want to excel"
- In 2018: "we hire only the best and the brightest"

Sounds more self-confident, doesn't it?

- In 2011, the company wanted to "give an impulse" to its clients' innovative and competitive strength
- In 2018, it also wanted to "contribute to the success" of its customers

A tad more entrepreneurial, I would say.

- In 2011, it wrote: "we hire people with a passion for engineering"

- In 2018, that ambition widened to "a passion for all aspects of technology"

That's definitely a wider passion.

- In 2011, TMC aimed for unspecified "growth"
- In 2018, it wanted growth a) in the existing business cells, b) by setting up new business cells for new niche markets, c) via international start-ups and d) possibly also via acquisitions

Now, is that more ambitious or not?

A 2019 CLIENT: SIETSKE VAN SCHAGEN (BOSCH)

When employeneur Ronald Cornelissen worked on the push-belt used in the Bosch continuous variable transmission, he did so in Tilburg, where Bosch Transmission Technology operates a production plant and a research and development unit. Combined, these have around 1,500 employees, mostly in production. Every year Bosch manufactures some eight million of these push-belts — each with four hundred links, in its factories in the Netherlands and Vietnam. The belts are sent to an assembly line in Mexico from which the completed transmission systems are shipped to vehicle manufacturers in Asia and the USA — just 1 percent goes to Europe.

In November 2019, I interviewed Sietske van Schagen, the team leader of the unit Ronald Cornelissen was a member of. Sietske, forty-one years old, studied chemical technology and industrial engineering at Saxion University of Applied Sciences in the city of Enschede. She worked as an account manager at a chemical company and became a process engineer at Bosch Transmission Technology in 2011. She briefly collaborated with Ronald — who began his placement at Bosch in 2012 — but was then transferred to a product development unit. Since September 2016, she's been the team lead in process development. "My team is responsible for the links in the push-belt, we do development projects and projects for process optimization," she explained. The team consists of sixteen engineers of whom five are external.[7]

The way it works at Bosch is that, when she has a vacancy in her team, she sends a note to the HR department, which in turn sends job profiles to a series of consultancies with preferred supplier statuses. "So I receive resumes from different sides." Other aspects of the contracting process are of no concern to her: Bosch works with standard job profiles, standard rates and a standard contract duration.

Bosch is an important customer for TMC. In 2019, eight of its engineers worked in Sietske's team, for various periods. Most stayed two to four years. "I think Ronald Cornelissen was even here for five years." That's because most of the process development team's projects are long term and complex. "It'll take you half a year before you really understand what we are doing. So I want people who are prepared to stay for a long time." When externally hired engineers leave, "it is rarely because they don't like their job anymore," she said. "Usually it's for personal reasons, like in Ronald's case," (who found his daily commuting time too burdensome).

So did Sietske see any differences between TMC and other high-tech and R&D consultancies? "In general, the providers from which we hire on a more regular basis have a good sense of the type of expertise that we need," she said. Yet, there are differences. "TMC clearly promotes employeneurship and I have regular discussions with them about training and courses." The distinctive point is not that TMC initiates these discussions. "As far as training is concerned, I treat our externals the same as internals, so in principle they get the same training and evaluations." However, unlike other providers, TMC likes to talk about the *kind* of training Bosch offers their employeneurs and about its relevance for their personal and professional development.

The interviewees in the 2017–2018 client feedback project didn't — and couldn't really — yet have a picture of TMC's internationalization strategy. A year and a half later, Sietske van Schagen had experienced at least one clear result of that strategy. "The expertise on thin sheet punching that I need is extremely hard to find in the

Netherlands. TMC was able to send me an Italian with a background in punching technology." (She didn't know whether TMC's Italian office had been involved in this candidacy). In general, she's hesitant about hiring foreigners. "I can't use people who stay for just a few months, they must be prepared to come for a longer period. So it's important that they are well supported, get help with finding lodging and some introduction to the Dutch culture." With the Italian expert, things worked out really well. He had already done another project in the Netherlands before coming to Bosch. "And I know that TMC has set up an expat community for its foreign employeneurs, which regularly organizes events and dinners."

From Sietske's point of view, TMC's cell structure is not by definition convenient. "I have TMC people from different cells, which means that I have to communicate with different account managers. Since it drives me crazy to keep them all informed, I pick one of them as my main contact." On the other hand, she is very satisfied with TMC's problem-solving abilities. "Last summer there was a problem with one of their employeneurs and when I asked them to help me, they did so quickly and really well." She remembered just one case in which a TMC employeneur didn't function well, a few years ago. "When someone dysfunctions, I use a four-stage approach. I indicate my dissatisfaction, then indicate it a second time. In stage three, I involved TMC. They quickly took action, in a very correct, decent way."

▌ THE CONVERSION PROBLEM

There's just one thing Sietske van Schagen doesn't like about the high-tech and R&D consultancy business: if she finds really, really good engineers, she can't keep them. She would like to convert some of them to her permanent payroll, but Bosch doesn't allow it, she said: "They don't want to expand their headcount."

Unlike ASML. In 2018, the number of TMC engineers deployed at the global leader in semiconductor production systems was around 180. Then ASML introduced a new flex policy. The member of the team who devised it was Hans Strieder, who helped set up TMC in its early

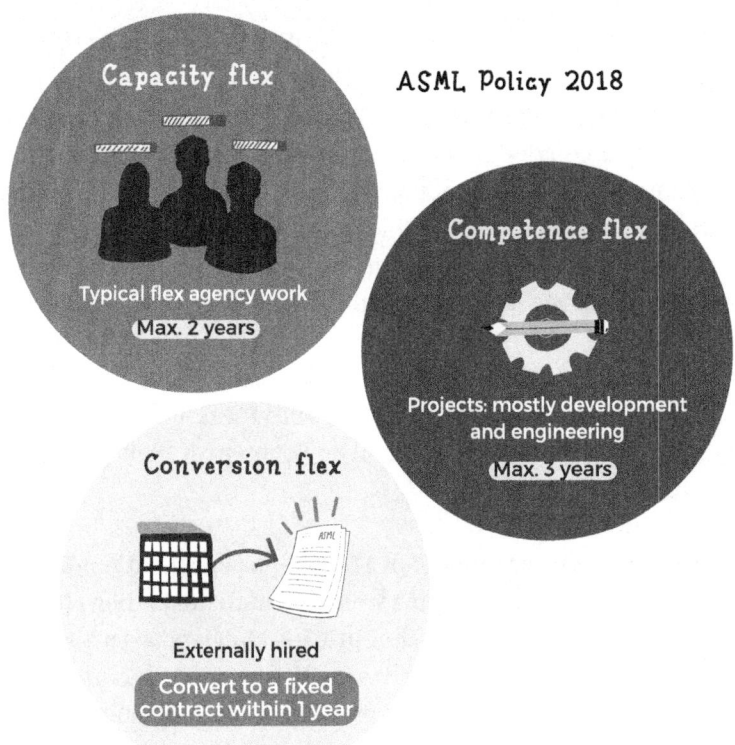

Capacity flex

ASML Policy 2018

Typical flex agency work

Max. 2 years

Competence flex

Projects: mostly development and engineering

Max. 3 years

Conversion flex

Externally hired

Convert to a fixed contract within 1 year

days and became "accessory" to a course of action that might seriously damage the creation of boyhood friend Thijs Manders. The new policy, which aimed to create more transparency but also to reduce the flex-force at the Veldhoven site, was implemented in early 2018. When I interviewed him in March 2019, the effects on TMC were fully visible.[8]

Strieder explained that ASML had organized its flexible workforce in three groups:

- capacity flex (typical flex agency work mostly seen in operations, for a maximum of two years, usually of technical staff with intermediate and higher vocational training)
- competence flex (typical for engineers/designers working in projects mostly in development and engineering, for a maximum of three years)
- conversion flex (engineers, externally hired with the purpose to convert to a fixed contract after a year)

The new flex policy implied the halving of the competences flex group from thirty to around fifteen percent and a parallel increase of the conversion flex group. It was inspired by ASML's commercial success and its conviction that its growth path would continue in the foreseeable future. From that point of view, expanding its permanent workforce and reducing its flexible layers made sense. But for TMC it was bad news because it also meant that ASML started to swallow up more TMC employeneurs and take them into its own workforce.

"I talked about it with Ronald van Gerwen, then CEO of TMC Netherlands," Strieder said. "TMC wrestled with the issue but decided to stick to their strategy of focusing on deployment of their people on competence flex level."[9]

By the end of 2018, the number of TMC employeneurs at ASML had gone down from a 170 to 55. This was of course a major blow (on a total of around eight hundred), but in Thijs Manders' eyes it was also a lack of recognition of TMC's significance for ASML. During our early 2019 interview he said: "We provided them continuity. When a TMC engineer finished a project at ASML, we transferred him to another client, such as TNO or Philips, but ultimately he would return to ASML." Put differently: TMC maintained a talent pool from which ASML could draw upon request. If the new policy weakened TMC, it would also weaken that talent pool.[10]

Was Manders being too pessimistic? Mostly due to ASML's policy, TMC's number of employeneurs in the Netherlands in 2018 had indeed ended below budget. Not by minus 115 but by 85, which implied that TMC had managed to at least partially compensate the loss of ASML business by finding new opportunities at other clients and by acquiring new clients. Moreover, the international expansion had paid off. TMC Belgium and the offices in Paris, Italy and Sweden, in particular, had shown considerable personnel growth. Only TMC Belgium and the Paris office had made a profit, but the future of the internationalization strategy looked promising. All in all, TMC group's profit had turned out at just under €13.1 million, which was slightly over the projected budget.[11]

AN EXCITING, YET DIFFICULT YEAR

Yet, 2019 became a difficult year. To begin with, the decline in TMC's placements at ASML interfered with the search for a new financial partner. At the end of 2017, TMC had received a participation offer from Ergon Capital, a Belgian investment group associated with Albert Frère's powerful Groupe Bruxelles Lambert (GBL) financial holding. TMC's financial majority partner Gilde Buy Out was interested. The fund had been involved with TMC for five years and was ready to exit. However, Gilde's management didn't want to enter into direct negotiations with Ergon Capital but preferred an auction type process, which would involve possible strategic partners (i.e. other high-tech and R&D consultancies) and other private equity groups. In September 2018, after reviewing TMC's (positive) financials for the second quarter, Gilde set the process in motion. "The response was enormous," Thijs Manders remembered during our early 2020 meeting. "Twenty-five parties were interested, TMC's value was estimated at €150–200 million."[12]

By the end of 2018, as the effect of ASML's new conversion policy became visible, this valuation faded, as did the number of interested parties. In the end, TMC chose Ergon Capital, which valued the group at around €100 million. Manders frankly admits that it took him a little while to swallow his disappointment about the lower valuation. But he remained convinced of the advantages of an alliance with Ergon Capital. The group was Belgian — as is Emmanuel Mottrie, who was leading the international expansion and had succeeded him as CEO in April 2018. A takeover by another high-tech and R&D consultancy like Altran or Randstad would inevitably have resulted in the disappearance of the TMC brand, which would now stay alive. Most importantly, Ergon vowed to support TMC's employeneurship model and the group's organic internationalization strategy.[13]

The deal was finalized on May 1, 2019, and — after gaining permission from the Dutch competition authorities — announced on June 20. Ergon Capital bought all shares in Time Acquisition, the legal entity that held all TMC shares, and created a new legal structure named Triple BV. The board of management, Emmanuel Mottrie and Rogier van Beek as well as the TMC founders Thijs Manders and Jan van Rijt all re-invested substantial parts of their proceeds. Part of the shares had been reserved for other management allowing them to benefit from the value creation. After the re-investment, Ergon retained a 66.8% of Triple BV (TMC).

Unfortunately, the group's growth lost momentum. Business in the Netherlands, which still represented seventy percent of all activities, continued to slow and revenue there, which had been budgeted to grow by six percent, instead fell by five percent. The France-Ouest office in Rennes was expected to more than double its revenue but instead saw it go down almost forty percent. To stop this downward trend, Emmanuel Mottrie decided to replace the local CEO and move the office to Nantes. Revenue in Belgium increased by over ten percent but had been budgeted to increase by twenty-five percent. Likewise, the offices in Spain and Portugal, Toulouse and France PACA (Provence, Alpes, Côte d'Azur) realized growth but less than hoped for. In North America, the office in Montreal, Canada, started in 2018, should have reached over €1 million in revenue but managed only half a million — which in itself wasn't too bad, really. But there was good news too: the Paris office exceeded expectations by generating more than fifty percent revenue growth; Italy grew over a hundred percent (and was almost on budget) and revenue in Sweden didn't grow sevenfold — as budgeted — but still more or less exploded with an over four hundred percent increase. Even the Dubai office, which had suffered from start-up problems in 2017–2018 and saw its CEO leave due to private circumstances, reached the break-even point. All in all, 37 percent of group revenue had been realized outside the Netherlands (and forty percent of its employeneurs were working abroad).[14]

Despite the various setbacks, the total picture for 2019 was better than in 2018. Total group revenue in 2018 had been almost €96 million and increased to almost €103 million; while earnings climbed from €12 to €12.5 million (EBITDA, discounting start-up investments). Many companies would be happy with seven percent revenue growth and five percent earnings growth. But TMC had aimed for twenty-five percent and almost thirty percent, respectively.[15]

So compared to that aim, 2019 offered a reality check, another one, about a decade after the first, which had resulted from the Adapté takeover in 2006 and the credit crisis of 2008. Were there parallels? Not that many. Unlike then, there hadn't been a major takeover, no financial overburdening, there weren't any serious "bleeders," there wasn't any need for depreciations or restructuring operations (except at the France Ouest office). In fact, the causes for the stagnation were mixed. When I met CFO Rogier van Beek in May 2020 he specifically mentioned the Dutch branch. "In general, the energy level in that branch wasn't perfect. The years before, things had gone so well that a certain complacency had slipped in. We should have reacted differently to the ASML conversion problem, less defensively and in a more anticipatory way." He also felt that the shift from Gilde to Ergon as a financial partner might have consumed quite a bit of management energy.[16]

To address those issues, the company made some changes at the cell management level in the Netherlands. And at the end of 2019, TMC Netherlands CEO Ronald van Gerwen left. On his LinkedIn page he wrote: "After almost twelve years, I have decided to resign and leave TMC. That wasn't an easy choice but when the passion starts to flow away, and work costs more energy than it produces, you have to be honest to your colleagues, your organization and above all to yourself. Then this is the appropriate choice."[17]

Van Gerwen ended his message with a thank you to his TMC colleagues and a happy new year. And indeed, 2019 might have ended in a minor key and some of TMC's foreign ambitions might have been too high, but there seemed no real reason to drastically scale down the long-term growth plans that had been developed during the 2018 transition year and which I shall discuss shortly.

However, in March 2020 the Covid-19 pandemic struck and changed the future.

CHAPTER 7

THE FUTURE

Hold on.

Before I get to the virus and its effects on TMC's future, I first need to describe what that future looked like before Covid-19. Because in TMC's eyes, it already had a clear shape.

READY TO GO

As mentioned before: in 2019 TMC — by growing 7.3 percent — passed the €100 million revenue mark, the exact figure being €102,658,000. That was no small feat. Despite the fact that the outcome was below budget, the mood on the board was good, CFO Rogier van Beek remembered when I met him in mid-2020. "We had tackled the problems that had surfaced in 2019 and were in very good flow again." Yes, to meet the targets of the three-year business plan the board had put on paper in 2018 would require some more time than expected. But there seemed no reason to adjust, discard or radically change it.[1]

Emmanuel Mottrie, too, continued to believe in the dream, of which the business plan was part. When I met him in March 2020, in the early days of the Covid crisis in Europe, he said, "We are very ambitious, we want to double in size in five years..." And then double again. And double again.[2]

THE DREAM AND THE PLAN

I intentionally use dream, not plan. A dream is a vision, sketchy, with broad views and far horizons. A plan is sharp, detailed, within range. In 2018, TMC had described both a dream *and* a plan. The dream was this: in the five years from 2018 to 2023, TMC would grow to 2,500 employeneurs; then to 5,000 by 2028; and then to 10,000 by 2033. The business plan covered the first three years of these fifteen. That was also the limit of the financial projections the board had made.[3]

The fifteen year expansion dream rested on seven pillars. One was a principle, five were in various phases of construction, the seventh would be totally new.

The Fifteen Year Expansion Dream

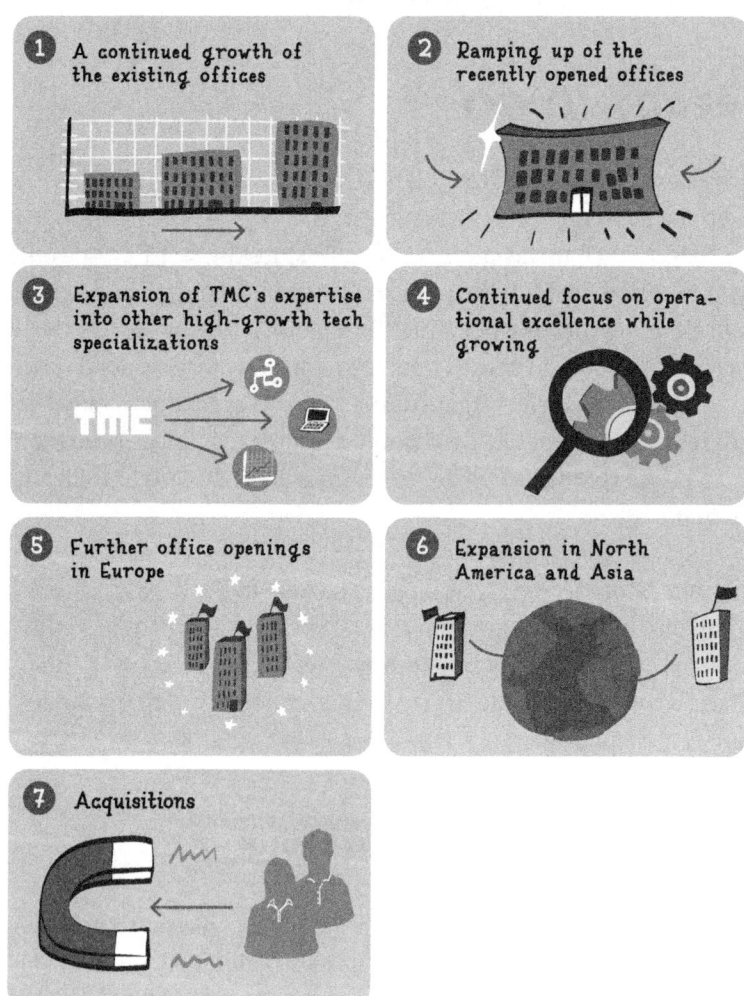

1 A continued growth of the existing offices

2 Ramping up of the recently opened offices

3 Expansion of TMC's expertise into other high-growth tech specializations

4 Continued focus on operational excellence while growing

5 Further office openings in Europe

6 Expansion in North America and Asia

7 Acquisitions

In more detail:[4]

1. Growth of existing offices

At that time, the offices in the Netherlands, Belgium and Paris were the main source centers of TMC's revenues and profit.

In the Netherlands, the possibilities for growth in the company's home region of Eindhoven and surroundings seemed limited. But there would be talent pools and business opportunities in the eastern region around Enschede, which has a quite entrepreneurial technical university and an interesting client base with manufacturing companies like TenCate and Nedap; and Wageningen University, which focuses on food and agriculture, can claim a very good international reputation and has close connections with large industrial groups like Unilever and FrieslandCampina (dairy foods). In addition, growth could be found in the Randstad region, where TMC had just opened an office in Delft, with its renowned mechatronics and aerospace oriented technical university; and would soon (i.e. 2019) open one in Utrecht, in the heart of the Netherlands, where science and industry have a distinct focus on life sciences (biotechnology, pharmaceutical R&D and clinical sciences).

In Belgium and Paris, TMC had built a substantial foothold with plenty of room for further expansion, the board felt, both by increasing the number of employeneurs at existing clients and by acquiring new clients.

2. Ramping up recently opened offices

... meaning the offices in Italy, Spain/Portugal, France other than Paris, Sweden, North America and Dubai in the United Arab Emirates. One of the main mechanisms to stimulate their growth would be to use TMC's contacts with existing multinational clients to place its employeneurs at their subsidiaries in these regions. This was already happening. In 2015, TMC had been serving five multinational clients in more than one country; that number had doubled in two years' time. The group also intended to work hard to become a supplier to Airbus, which was hiring thousands of external R&D personnel.

The key to this ramping up process, TMC felt, was the recruitment power of its disruptive, transparent employeneurship model. By that time, the model had shown that it didn't just appeal to engineers in the Netherlands but in other countries as well. Given the high demand for technical talent all across Europe, North America and Asia, there would be many opportunities for a high-tech and R&D consultancy which was able to attract and retain such talent.

3. Expand into other high-growth tech niches

As described earlier, at the end of 2017, TMC had eighteen cells. It had particularly high expectations of the cells that were focusing on industrial automation, life sciences and data science cells. Their growth would be driven by several trends, the board felt: the need for continuous cost reduction in manufacturing, increased expenditures in health care, and the rise of big data in decision-making processes.

For the future, TMC saw opportunities in new specializations like manufacturing 4.0 (the next step in industrial automation, driven by "cyber-physical" [robot] systems), biotechnology (driven by the health care industry), artificial intelligence and pharmaceuticals.

On top of all this, the board expected that the technology executives cell, set up in 2017 by Katja Pahnke and still in its infancy, would in fact profit from an increasing need for senior executives with a strong technological background. In its view, the most senior employeneurs, who had built up experience as sparring partners for both engineering specialists and top managers, would be ideal candidates for such positions. During our March 2020 meeting, Emmanuel Mottrie warned against exaggerating expectations of this cell, though. "Since we started it, it has been relatively small and that will not really change." According to Mottrie, it is not difficult to find suitable people for the role of technology executive. "We are regularly contacted by experienced managers at the age of fifty, fifty-five, who have been sidelined or are being regarded as too expensive by their employer, but still want a new challenge and have the energy for it. Our model is a perfect fit for them." In the TMC model, they will have to accept some more insecurity and risk than they are used to, but financially they may even benefit. While their fixed salary will be lower than in their previous job, the TMC profit sharing bonus may actually bring them to a higher income level, Mottrie said.[5]

4. A continued focus on operational excellence

This may sound self-evident but by giving it the status of a pillar the TMC board proved that it was aware of the organizational pitfalls of growing. It would be challenging to maintain the employeneurship model and the present low-cost governance structure, even if the organization itself became five times — and eventually ten — times larger. In the board's view this required a focus on maintaining TMC's flat organizational structure; the use of smart technology to centralize financial and fiscal management; and a continued focus on stimulating an entrepreneurial mindset. Part of that stimulus would consist of a TMC Opportunity Wall, an online platform to help employeneurs choose from the growing pool of projects at international customers. Another element would be the introduction of financial stimuli for national and regional office managers to co-operate in the search for candidates, clients and projects (TMC Square).[6]

Emmanuel Mottrie has clear ideas about operational excellence, which in his view depends to a large extent upon organizational excellence. "We have a decentralized organization," he said, "with a maximum of autonomy and a high level of entrepreneurship. We can only maintain that model if we manage to expand the organization along those lines. To do that, we will have to introduce entirely new forms of organization that are based on shared values like transparency and solidarity." That will be a formidable task, he felt. "Many of our employeneurs come from corporate backgrounds that offered them bad organizational examples. Despite the fact that they left these backgrounds and chose TMC, some of them tend to fall back into their old inertia. The same happens to some of our managers who still tend to treat employeneurs as subordinates instead of as owners of their own destinies." Even with TMC's extensive personal and professional development programs, the assistance of coaches and the explicit focus on the 5Q model, keeping the company's core values as alive and inspiring as they have been in the past decade will have to be a permanent point of focus, he feels. It would make sense, of course, to put the office directors, cell directors and business managers in charge of this value maintenance task. Mottrie realized that. "It is important to offer your employeneurs not just interesting projects, and personal and professional development but also possibilities to grow and develop within the TMC organization and thus breed entrepreneurial people who can set up new offices and cells."[7]

***

Pillars one to four were also part of TMC's 2018–2021 business plan, which aimed at an expansion from around 800 direct FTEs (employeneurs) at the end of 2018 to around 1,070 at the end of 2021 in the established offices in the Netherlands, Belgium and Paris; and an expansion from around 65 to 460 FTEs in the recently opened international offices in the same period — leading to a total target of 1,530.

To reach that target, projected growth in the first of these three years, 2019, should have been to 1,100 FTEs. As will be clear from my account about the developments in that year, TMC didn't reach that level. The real direct FTE figure at the end of 2019 was about 990, some 40 FTEs higher than end 2018 (indirect FTEs grew by just 6).

Growth pillars five, six and seven were beyond the range of the business plan, the board saw these as the crucial steps to accelerate growth in the remainder of the 2020s, up until 2033.[8]

5. Further office openings in Europe

Between organic growth and acquisitions there is of course another step: setting up additional greenfield offices. It was a strategy that had proven its viability in the previous years: in 2019 revenues from TMC's international operations went up from twenty-five percent to thirty-seven percent, and EBITDA results from twenty-five to almost thirty percent (excluding start-up investments).[9]

Additional offices would be feasible in France, Sweden and Switzerland, and in the mid-term also in Finland and Germany, according to the 2018 strategy document. In France, the new offices might focus on the automotive, chemical and pharmaceutical industries; in Sweden on a wide variety of R&D institutes and high-tech companies.

Finland would be interesting for its telecom industry, Germany for — of course — automotive and aerospace; Switzerland for its pharma and life science industries.[10]

When I met him in March 2020, Emmanuel Mottrie sounded somewhat more cautious about the start-up possibilities in Germany and Switzerland than the 2018 strategic dream. "Their consultancy markets are highly regulated," he said. "You need licenses, which is a rather complex affair. So probably the best way will be to acquire consultancies that already have these licenses."[11]

Another problem about entering the German market will be the "very conservative and hierarchical corporate culture," Mottrie added. "They are much less open to flexible labor and hiring external expertise/competences than in other European countries. Newly graduated top engineers prefer to work directly for companies like Siemens, Porsche or Bosch rather than join a consultancy." Since this limits the possibilities for high-tech and R&D consultancy in the top market segment — in the strategic core of the client — TMC decided to search for a technology consultancy in the middle market segment (described earlier in this book as "specialized recruitment services, usually for filling positions that require specific — but not high-end — expertise"). "The idea is to find an existing group in that segment with about ten offices across Germany and then expand that to about a hundred FTEs per office," he said.[12]

6. Expansion in North America and Asia

When the board wrote down its dream, back in 2018, TMC had in fact just made its first moves in these two continents by opening offices in Montreal, Canada and Dubai, in the United Arab Emirates. The first was in preparation of a next step, towards the USA (New York and Seattle); Dubai in preparation of a step to Hong Kong and Shanghai, China's high-tech centers. The step to New York City followed in 2019, when TMC rented a small office on West 33d Street in midtown Manhattan, not far from Penn Station, and hired a tiny staff to set it up, under the supervision of Fernando Ledesma, formerly a consultant at Altran, Randstad and Akka, who also ran the Montreal office. Beginning a greenfield high-tech and R&D consultancy in the super-competitive New York City environment wasn't easy. Maybe you remember meeting Prenella Patterson from the NY office at the TMC's Fundamentals session in November 2019. She acquired a master's degree in finance and worked in risk management and in the transportation and automotive industry before joining TMC at the end of July 2019. During the workshop, some four months later, she conceded that she hadn't yet managed to bring in any customers. "I had been sure that I'd find the first one within a month. So I was a little disappointed and heartbroken. But my boss said: hey, don't worry, you'll have highs and lows, you can bring them in. So I continued laying the groundwork and building contacts with potential clients." Soon Prenella's boss — Thomas Vilmer — was proved right: in Augustus 2020 the New York office had placed fifteen employeneurs, and had reached break-even point.[13]

The Dubai venture, started in 2017, took longer before it began to generate revenue. As described earlier, the first CEO had to resign for personal reasons. In addition, the Dubai bureaucracy wasn't particularly helpful. It took TMC until early 2019 to get a bank account, which is of course essential to do business. In February 2019, the company found a new CEO, Jonathan Petit, who worked for the French high-tech and R&D consultancy Akka, including six years in Dubai, before joining TMC. From that moment on, and with the bank account in place, things started to roll. In August 2020, the Dubai office was deploying around ten employeneurs and performing a little over budget.[14]

In the 2018 strategy document, TMC wrote that it expects the employeneurship model to land well in both North America and Asia. If Prenella Patterson's enthusiasm and the first results of the New York and the Dubai offices are an indication, the future indeed looks promising — although the 2020 Covid-19 crisis made it impossible to predict any time frame for further developments.

7. Acquisitions

As Emmanuel Mottrie formulated it in our March 2020 meeting, "We will not be able to realize our ambitions with just organic growth, so we will also actively explore the possibilities for acquisitions." He was well aware of TMC's apprehension on this issue, due to the failed 2006 Adapté takeover. So he added, "If we buy something, it will be a relatively small firm that is open to our culture and able to adapt to it."[15]

In the 2018 strategy document, the board had taken the same position: "An essential starting point in evaluating any acquisition is that the culture of the target fits TMC's employeneurship model. Other important criteria are true entrepreneurial leadership and small to medium-sized target (ten to forty direct FTEs)." The document specifically mentioned Switzerland as a possible target country. TMC already has a number of Swiss and Switzerland-based — mainly pharmaceutical — firms as clients in other countries. It would make sense to buy a Swiss consultancy that was already serving these same firms in Switzerland. Since 2018, the board has also been considering an acquisition in Germany, for reasons that Emmanuel Mottrie explained earlier (see pillar 5).[16]

▋ THE COVID-19 CRISIS

On March 11, 2020, the World Health Organization designated the outbreak of Covid-19 as a pandemic. The coronavirus causing this respiratory disease — SARS-CoV2 — had been spreading across the globe for several months, the death toll was rising and, worldwide, authorities reacted with increasingly restrictive measures including complete "lockdowns," stay-at-home orders and economic shutdowns.

I met with Emmanuel Mottrie two days earlier, on March 9. Earlier that day, the Italian prime minister Giuseppe Conte had declared a code red situation for his entire country. "I just spoke to our CEO in Milan," Mottrie said. "We have seventy employeneurs there. Fortunately, all of them — except three — can continue to work." Yet, he was worried. The Amadeus IT Group, for example, an important producer of ticketing software for airline reservation systems, was suffering from the collapse of air travel and had put all new development projects on hold. As a result, Amadeus' development center in Sofia Antipolis, in the south of France, wouldn't be hiring any new software experts — a step that would frustrate the growth of TMC's young office in that region. "And in Belgium," he added as another example, "we have a client in semiconductors with a lot of business in China. Like Amadeus, they have already lost thirty percent of their revenues. Their CEO has said: for the time being, no more consultancy. So it's hard to say where we're going. One thing seems certain: our plans will suffer delays."[17]

These were the early days of the lockdown period. On March 11, the day of the WHO's pandemic declaration, the Dutch government issued its own set of "intelligent" lockdown measures, which included a stay-at-home call, a work-at-home call and — four days later — the closure of schools and restaurants. Twelve weeks later, on June 4, I met with TMC's CFO Rogier van Beek, who gave me an extensive picture of his own, the board's and TMC's reaction to the Covid-19 crisis.

The power of transparency and solidarity

The crisis, Van Beek began by saying, came as a complete shock. "After the measures we'd taken in the fall of 2019, we were in a very good flow again. So when corona came, it was as if we were in the middle of a party and suddenly someone switched on the lights."[18]

The board's first focus was on taking care of the people. "Some of them got into an emotional cramp. So you have to 'uncramp' them. Emmanuel and I formed a small crisis team, consisting of ourselves and two assistants, and began to think of ways to keep the employeneurs who were now at home — either working or 'on the bench' — connected, using technologies like Teams. Then we picked up the phone. Every day, we randomly called business managers, office managers and country CEOs. We didn't do that to send a message but to listen and answer questions, and to talk, not just about the business but also about their private situation. By doing so, we learned very much about the physical situation, the well-being and the state of mind of our people and their families."

"On the financial side, we opened our credit lines, maximized governmental subsidies in all countries and determined which investments could be postponed. The major goal was to safeguard employment for everybody, without touching people's net income. Other consultancies were lowering salaries, but we felt that would be against our core values." TMC also continued paying regular expenses, such as for travel and coaching, kept the bonus system in place and made sure no one would wind up in a negative bonus situation. "And of course we also listened carefully to our customers and thought along with them on how to deal with this situation."

"At a later stage," he said, "both Emmanuel and me started inviting some of our people to our homes, to eat a simple lunch — fried eggs and toast — and talk." That wasn't some kind of trick, he emphasized, not something they had conceived or read in a crisis management handbook. "It's just who we are. It's the family feeling." The idea basically originated in his own fear. "Of course I personally had concerns too, but then, one weekend, I sat down and considered the situation. And I thought, what can go wrong? I have always believed in the robustness of the business model and the strategy." After a while, this line of thinking quieted him down, he said.

The key of his and Mottrie's handling of the Covid-19 crisis has been transparency, Van Beek said. To all those involved: employeneurs, other employees, shareholders, banks. "We invited the employee council every week, talked with the shareholders every week, with the cell directors every week." Because Ronald van Gerwen, the CEO of TMC Netherlands had left the company just a few months earlier, and had not yet been replaced, Van Beek and Mottrie took over his responsibilities on a temporary basis. "Every week, we organized an online update session for our internal employees and twice we held a question and answer chat session for all our employeneurs. We tell them everything we do, about the financial situation, about our discussions with the banks, I literally showed them the slides I showed the banks." The point is, he said, "If you are transparent and show people the context within which they are now acting, they understand very well what part they have to play. You take them seriously. It motivates them to think along." And it elicits compliments, he added during a short follow-up interview in September 2020. "Yesterday, I had a proactive meeting with our banks. One of them, Rabobank, praised our transparency compared to other companies."[19]

▎ "NOW WE WILL PRESS AHEAD!"

So how did TMC's business develop during the first six months of the crisis? It could have been worse. In H1 total revenue and EBITDA profit were slightly below budget, i.e. slightly below the 2019 level. In the Netherlands, revenue was only three percent lower than budget and reported adjusted EBITDA was even higher than the initial budget. Also for the whole group, the COVID impact on revenues remained limited; total adjusted EBITDA was around five percent below the originally budgeted level.[20]

Across the entire group, the number of employeneurs (around 970) was just slightly lower than at the end of 2019 (around 990) till a little above the Q1 2019 level. The biggest problem was the percentage of employeneurs without a project, in TMC lingo: VIP (*vrij in project*, or free in project). The normal level, caused by transfers from one project to another, would be around five percent. Now it was some ten percent on average in H1 in the Netherlands and thirteen percent in the group. Most of the costs were still covered by the government relief measures. But this would be temporary. "So have we handled it until now? Yes," Van Beek said. "And is it a breathtaking situation? Of course."[21]

"The main question," Van Beek added, "is to take a position towards a crisis like this. And we have said: hell, now we will press ahead! From 2019, we still had a list of things to handle: a few underperformers, an office that needed some attention. So we set these unfinished things straight. And then we said: now we are going to use the crisis to our advantage. We see, for example, that the crisis causes great insecurity among self-employed high-tech and R&D consultants, who now discover that they aren't as entrepreneurial as they thought. These are highly trained people, technicians, who thought they could manage their careers on their own. As a result of the crisis, they are now much more open to joining us than before. And of course our model — with its combination of security and entrepreneurship — is exactly what they need. So we began to approach them."[22]

"The point is, we don't want to sit here in sackcloth and ashes. We don't want to talk crisis but look ahead. We want to put a dot on the horizon and to switch on our double-up plan as soon as the crisis fades. We want to exit the crisis stronger than we entered it. And that means: form a recruitment reservoir of four hundred candidates worldwide to whom we offer contracts that will be activated as soon as the projects start coming in again. We call that reservoir Two Must Connect — as you will note: TMC. Those projects may come in October, they may come in December, but when things start rolling again, we want to have the people for them."[23]

Meanwhile, Mottrie and Van Beek were talking with their key account managers about the prospects of the main clients and with the shareholders about new specializations and possible acquisitions. "You have to continue to think big," Van Beek said. And he concluded, "All we have to do is make sure we have good people. Then, the projects will come too."

Think Big

So in a way, after twenty years, the TMC circle is now complete. Van Beek's remark of "thinking big" is unmistakably an echo of Thijs Manders' attitude in the early days of the company — which, as the reader may remember, was born in the midst of a crisis. It is in times of crisis that a person's true character will inevitably show itself. Maybe the same can be said of companies. How do they behave during a life-threatening crisis? What actions do they take? What principles do they stick to? How do they adapt? To what extent are they able to see the new opportunities the crisis may offer? History is full of examples of businesses that lacked the character to survive disaster and severe setback, or only managed to do so by reverting to foul play. But there are also many that did show resilience and inventiveness, and came out stronger.

Will TMC be one of those strong, long-term survivors? It is impossible to predict the future, but the past offers two clear indications that they surely can be. The company managed both the 2001 and the 2009 crisis admirably well — with some bruises and scars, but with no lasting damage to speak of. The "now we will press ahead" attitude reflects the one Thijs Manders chose in 2001: not defensive but offensive and adaptive. That approach can at the very least be interpreted as a promising one.

ON THE ART OF ADAPTABILITY
Some real experiments and thought experiments

"Looking to the future, I think it will become ever more important in this century to have what they call '21st century skills' — the most important being, in my view, adaptability, and especially so in the world of technology."[24]

It is November 13, 2019, no Covid-19 crisis in sight yet, and I'm sitting in a restaurant, talking with Lotte Geertsen, the director of TMC's Entrepreneurial Lab, and Marjolein Berkers, at the time director incubators TMC Netherlands and interim-director of TMC's Chemical cell. Both are full of passion about TMC's future, the discussion covers a wide range of subjects. Lotte Geertsen has set the tone by calling her Entrepreneurial Lab "the superlative of employeneurship" and now launches into the 21st century skills theme and the need for adaptability. In her view, one of the directions in which TMC will/should gradually develop is towards becoming a Technology House. "Big companies are perfectly able to develop their own innovation programs and decide what external expertise they need to hire for implementing it. For small and medium-sized enterprises (SMEs) that is not so easy. TMC could consider helping them by not just deploying one expert to one project but by offering assistance in setting up a complete, bespoke innovation program, including a horizontal, multidisciplinary, cross-cell team of experts, composed of employeneurs from various relevant business cells, to implement it."

Then Berkers joins the discussion. "We might even go one step further," she says, "and participate financially in such a program. To step into it for better or worse, and co-invest. I can see that happening too."

In fact, this "co-creation" approach is already taking shape. Geertsen and Berkers point to Nanovations, a service TMC has devised to help organizations innovate using nanotechnology. The idea is that TMC will first help the client to identify his technological need and will then set up a team to take care of the entire R&D and implementation process until the phase of business development. As we speak, Nanovations is still in its infancy, as yet no concrete project has been finalized, but the first experiments have been set in motion.

Another future-oriented idea is to use The Entrepreneurial Lab for co-development of new products, in a joint venture with a client. "We call this: innovation as a service," Lotte Geertsen says. "Our offer is: dear client, dear partner, let's take each other by the hand and do this together. We will cover the initial development costs and as we move on and the road ahead becomes clearer, you step in too — until ultimately, we become co-investors." Again, as we speak the first experiments are being set up, in this case with a technology to 3D-print artificial teeth.

The innovation as a service concept (which had not yet officially started at the time of the interview) is closely connected to the purpose of The Entrepreneurial Lab, Geertsen adds. "We want our lab projects to aim at developing technology-based solutions to real world problems. By doing that, we challenge our employeneurs to ask themselves 'who has this problem?' and 'where is the demand for this product?' right from the start. By training them to think like that, and to experiment with those thoughts, you also train their adaptability to changing contexts and circumstances."

As our meeting approaches its end, I ask Berkers and Geertsen whether the TMC model, in their view, might be suitable in other sectors, outside the high-tech development world. Could be, they answer. Again, efforts to explore these possibilities are already underway. "We just organized a weekend session about innovation with a home care organization," Lotte Geertsen says. And Marjolein Berkers adds, "We did some initial reconnaissance and based on that, we think the employeneurship model might be useful for specialized nursing or legal services. As yet, these have only been thought experiments, but in my view the model can be used in any sector."

While discussing all this, I suddenly wonder to what extent TMC's clients might become inspired by the employeneurship model and might want to adopt certain elements of it to stimulate their employees' entrepreneurial spirit, their need to develop themselves professionally and personally, their adaptability. In sum, their "21st century skills?" Berkers and Geertsen chew on this. "It is true, at TMC we are very good at developing human capital," they say. "And some of the clients that hire our technological expertise could use some more of that human capital development expertise as well." It would be exciting to explore a move in that direction, they feel, to add human capital development as a new, next-level expertise to TMC's present and future technological specializations. "It's a bold idea, but I would welcome it," Berkers says, "to see TMC, in the next ten years, become an organization that deploys its employeneurship to help other organizations at all levels: in their operations, on a tactical level, on a strategic level." Ten months later, in September 2020, a first step in that direction was taken. TMC's Entrepreneurial Lab and the Pontes (coaching) Group started a joint project at one of TMC's clients to help make the client's organization and people more entrepreneurial.[25]

IN FOR THE LONG RUN...

A JOURNEY THROUGH THE LAND OF TMC

Before putting down my pen, I'd like to reflect a few moments on my journey through the land of TMC. I must admit that at the outset, I was skeptical. The TMC people I met during my first preparatory encounters, in late 2018, showered me with enthusiasm and with TMC lingo about "the model," "employeneurship," the "five pillars," "transparency" and the other terms you've become acquainted with. Of course they will be positive about their company, the professional researcher and author in me said. It's their baby, their world, their livelihood. And at first glance it seems to be doing well. But what will I find when I take a look inside?

Now I know.

So what's your final judgment? you may ask. Well, I have no final judgment. The Member Company is an on-going experiment, a project on the move. I can only offer some concluding observations.

RESILIENCE

One thing is clear. TMC has proven to be no mayfly. What struck me during the research is that the company is remarkable at maneuvering through crisis. It was born in one (the dot.com implosion of 2000–2001), was hit by a second one towards the end of its first decade (the 2008–2009 global financial crisis) and faced a third one while preparing its 20th anniversary (the Covid-19 crisis). To all of these three it reacted most of all intelligently. Often, in times of crises, executives will either freeze and wait too long to act or hit the brakes and start indiscriminate cost-cutting exercises. Thijs Manders (CEO in 2001 and 2009) and his successor Emmanuel Mottrie (CEO since 2019) chose a different approach. They mobilized what they call the company's central assets: its human capital and its value system.

I've found this to be not idle words but an engrained attitude. In the 2009 crisis, sharp cost cutting by TMC's major client ASML and problems at TMC's own Adapté subsidiary made a reduction of employeneur numbers unavoidable. As described in chapter 2, Manders and his supervisory board chose a combination of quick action at Adapté and decentralization of the group structure. The latter step, in particular, was not so much cost driven but rather stemmed from the conviction that TMC's cell structure had become overgrown by a top-heavy management layer. The organization had to go back to its basics, the cell structure had to become leading again.

Likewise, TMC's reaction to the Covid-19 crisis was value driven. When I interviewed chief financial officer Rogier van Beek at the height of the crisis, in June 2020, he immediately started talking about how Emmanuel Mottrie and he had first tried to make sure that "our people" were all right and felt taken care of. He pursued that subject for well over an hour before I finally had the chance to ask him about the group's financial situation — of which he briefly said, "We had to mobilize all our resources but we'll manage." (His brevity didn't conceal any intention to avoid the subject, he did give me some details of his financial measures.) Some months later, the figures for H1 confirmed his statement: TMC was navigating through the Covid-19 crisis pretty well.

So both these crises provided pretty convincing evidence that TMC indeed has a talent for crisis management. Which is an important quality. After researching and writing about companies — small, medium-sized and large — for over thirty years, I'm convinced that flexibility, adaptability and resilience are crucial for the lifespan of an organization, be it a commercial or a public one. To historians, this may sound like a no-brainer. Examples of societies, empires and cultures that vanished into oblivion during the lifetime of mankind abound. That is true, but often it seems that we learn little from them. As far as I can see, Thijs Manders and the people he surrounded himself with do not belong to the non-learners. They didn't just survive two crises but seem well on their way to survive the third one as well.

A STAUNCH BELIEF IN PROGRESS AND HUMAN POTENTIAL

To understand where TMC's survival skills and its continued focus on human capital and values come from, one has to remember that it was founded by people who i) were born in the (affluent) mid-1960s; ii) grew up in a high-tech, industrial environment; and iii) were interested in sociology and psychology. The similarities between their backgrounds and those of many of the major entrepreneurs in Silicon Valley are plentiful (except that there are no beaches and surfing waves in the Eindhoven region). Like their Californian peers, Thijs Manders, Hans Strieder, Freek van Bedaf and the TMC people of the first hour were staunch believers in technological progress and human potential. They had no doubt that societies can move forward in terms of technology and prosperity and that people have the ability to grow, both as professionals and as individual human beings. But they also knew that progress and development don't come for free, don't follow linear paths and can be interrupted by a crisis. In their own youth and early career years, they had experienced two global energy crises (1973 and 1979), two global recessions (early 1980s and early 1990s) and even one global health crisis (the HIV pandemic, which started in the 1980s).

It is this dual history that shaped them and gave them the ideas and convictions on which they built their company, and I'm sure they will agree if I say that in their view, the purpose of life is to create and to develop: things, technologies, organizations, people, oneself.

A FORWARD-LOOKING, NON-HIERARCHICAL, ANTI-MANAGERIAL CULTURE

As a result, TMC has rather distinct qualities. Most of all, it doesn't feel like an adult company. At the age of twenty, it still radiates the energy, enthusiasm, entrepreneurship, external orientation, flexibility and group spirit of the start-up. I admit that my impressions have been influenced by the interviews with directors of foreign subsidiaries. These are young and much more in a start-up mood than the Dutch mother. Yet, at TMC's headquarters, too, the visitor will not find an atmosphere of "adult" complacency, nor find symbols of functional differences, status or hierarchy, such as extra luxurious offices for top management.

This clearly is a forward-looking company. Beside the entrance, where other companies would display their products and history, TMC has positioned its Entrepreneurial Lab, in full view. The only references to history are quotes from technological geniuses of all ages on the walls throughout the building.

It is also a "flat," non-hierarchical company. Yes, there is a receptionist at the front door and, yes, the CEO has an assistant, but he will walk to the coffee machine for you and push the buttons himself. This lack of pomp suits a company which boasts a decentralized organizational structure, financial participation of country CEOs, far-reaching internal financial transparency towards its employeneurs (and towards me as the author of this book) et cetera. When I asked Emmanuel Mottrie in one of our final phone calls if he would call the TMC culture "anti-managerial." He said, "Yes, being a manager is not good enough in this company, we need entrepreneurial people."

Mottrie is convinced that it will be possible to maintain TMC's decentralized, entrepreneurial culture even if the company grows to ten thousand employeneurs, as is its ambition. How? By sticking to the people-driven, value-driven principles of the organization that drove the founders and that are driving the "entrepreneurial" non-managers they have attracted thus far.

This is in fact one of the few issues about which I remain skeptical. Remember Eckart Wintzen. He maintained the cell structure and family culture of his BSO company for twenty (!) years, but after his retirement it quickly faded and entirely disappeared after BSO was acquired by the much bigger multinational Atos group. In 2011, Thijs Manders and his supervisory board at that time rejected an acquisition offer that would have propelled TMC into a similar process. It will be interesting to see what will happen if another financially powerful buyer presents itself someday (since the group is not publicly listed, a hostile takeover would be impossible, but a voluntary one isn't).

A REVALUATION OF TECHNOLOGY, ENGINEERING AND MANUFACTURING

When talking to TMC executives, board members and employeneurs, and hearing about all their projects, one cannot fail to note that the Netherlands is in fact quite technology-minded. More than it's aware of. Its self-image still is that of a trading nation with a large agricultural sector and a few huge industrial multinationals — the biggest of which are in fact Anglo-Dutch. Since the recessions of the early 1980s and early 1990s, which mainly hit traditional manufacturing sectors, most Dutch people — and most of the media — no longer regard their country as industrial, let alone as high-tech and R&D-oriented. TMC exemplifies the opposite notion. As I've written earlier in this book, its engineers are on the frontline of many futuristic, state-of-the-art technological developments. The company came to fruition at the center of a Schumpeterian process of "creative destruction" and technological rejuvenation, which started around 1990 and resulted in the dismantling of the old Philips Incandescent Works and the rise of dozens of split-offs and spin-offs, some of which have become electronics giants of their own (ASML, NXP).

By focusing on the technological core of its clients and by offering its people tools to develop both their hard and their soft skills, TMC has stimulated the breeding of a new, less-nerdy type of engineer: one who is highly professional but is also capable of participating in — and even leading — project teams. By doing so, the company has definitely contributed to the revaluation of the engineering profession in the Netherlands, which had suffered much loss of status during the de-industrialization phase of the late 20th century. For a long time, being an engineer in the Netherlands would not bring one much public appreciation. Those days have changed, and may change even more once the general Dutch public and media become more aware of the huge economic potential of the nation's high-tech industries. It wouldn't surprise me if the Covid-19 crisis and the increasingly dramatic consequences of climate change stimulate this process in the coming decades.

A "LOCALIZED" INTERNATIONAL-IZATION STRATEGY

Finally, I'm downright impressed by TMC's internationalization strategy and the way the company is implementing it. By setting up low-cost greenfield operations it has managed to realize a pretty fast expansion. By simultaneously refraining from costly acquisitions (one failure at home apparently was enough), it appears to succeed in creating a level of cultural unity of subsidiaries in — at the time of writing — three continents and with employeneurs of many nationalities. That is no small feat. Part of it can no doubt be attributed to the nature of its activity: modern high technology is of course universal in principle, and engineering is probably one of the most globalized businesses in the world. But the interviews in this book show that the pillars of the TMC model are like the strings of a universal instrument on which one can produce pleasant chords for a variety of national ears.

THE WISDOM OF INSECURITY

Remember the Introduction? Remember philosopher Alan Watts and his ideas about mankind's search for stability in vulnerable and uncertain times, as put down in his book *The Wisdom of Insecurity*? Remember how he wrote that the art of living in such times requires "being completely sensitive to each moment, in regarding it as utterly new and unique, in having the mind open and wholly receptive?" Watts was referring to individual openness and individual sensitivity. So did employeneurship theorist Freek van Bedaf when he talked about XQ, executional intelligence, as one's self-propelling capacity. Clearly, the early 21st century is as vulnerable as it gets: full of volatility, uncertainty, complexity and ambiguity. Sensitivity to the moment and open-mindedness are more important than ever. So how can we rate TMC as a group on the XQ scale? Does it possess the intelligences and the executive power to handle these VUCA times? I guess the answer must be: yes, so far. But as everyone knows, past successes offer no guarantee for the future. To paraphrase Watts' words: the wisdom of insecurity requires the acceptance that each moment will be utterly new and unique.

POSTSCRIPT JANUARY 15, 2021

The final copy for this book was written in the summer of 2020, in the midst of the Covid-19 crisis. On the previous pages you have read how TMC reacted to that crisis. Now, with all the lay-out and correction work finished and just before printing, I asked CFO Rogier van Beek how TMC did in the remainder of 2020.

He reported that the number of employeneurs declined slightly in the summer but rebounded in Q4, particularly in the Netherlands, Belgium and Italy. As a result, the total number of employeneurs at year's end was even up somewhat on the previous year: 1179 compared to 1163 (headcount), or in FTEs: 998 compared to 990.

Despite the intensity and duration of the crisis, TMC managed to keep turnover at the 2019 level and even increased its profitability by 7 percent.

TMC continues to invest, Van Beek added. On January 1, 2021, the company started new business cells for telecom and supply chain management. It opened an office in Groningen (in the north of the Netherlands) and plans to open new offices in various European countries. It has hired around fifteen new business managers (in part as replacement but also in view of the expansion the company aims for in 2021) and is intensifying its online recruitment activities.

ACKNOWLEDGEMENTS

The great majority of companies that have their histories recorded cannot resist the urge to control every detail of the research process and, most of all, to control every word of the publication. TMC's founder Thijs Manders and the board were different. They gave me ample space to develop my own plan, to conduct my own research and to write down my findings in words of my own choosing; in TMC terminology: to go on my own journey through the company. To underscore their self-confidence and their trust in my approach, they accepted my condition that I hold the copyright. The fact that this book is published under my own name is proof that they have taken this right seriously and have been able to respect my independence as author until the end. This is a remarkable, exceptional attitude, for which I'm grateful and which — by the way — fully supports their claim of corporate transparency.

TMC's employeneurs in the Netherlands and other countries proved equally transparent. They were glad to share their stories and did not shy away from talking about difficult moments in their careers. I thank all of them for their openness and their availability.

I'm especially grateful to Freek van Bedaf of Pontes Group. He gave me access to a series of internal documents which detail the way he anchored the employeneurship concept to accomplish theories of personality and motivation, and the way he developed the employeneurship assessment procedure.

This wasn't a solo project. Beatrix Broekmans and Krijn Schramade did a series of excellent interviews and reports. The TMC staff — particularly Marjolein Berkers, Lotte Geertsen and Stephanie Prins — were very helpful in organizing the research and fact-checking process.

A final word of thanks goes out to professors Ger Post and Mathieu Weggeman who gave important feedback on my initial plan and on the draft text, and offered valuable suggestions for improvement of the latter.

Marcel Metze
Ooij, the Netherlands, September 2020.

NOTES

INTRODUCTION

1   Watts: https://en.wikipedia.org/wiki/Alan_Watts — accessed January 23, 2020.
2   VUCA: https://en.wikipedia.org/wiki/Volatility,_uncertainty,_complexity_and_ambiguity — accessed January 23, 2020. Quote derived from A. Watts, The Wisdom of Insecurity: A Message for an Age of Insecurity, Random House e-book, accessed from https://bit.ly/38zmMX4, January 23, 2020.
3   TMC 2018–2020 financials, internal document provided by CFO Rogier van Beek.

1   START SMALL, THINK BIG

1   Interview with Hans Strieder, March 20, 2019.
2   Interviews with Thijs Manders, February 26, 2019 and January 28, 2020.
3   Thijs Manders, February 2019. He explicitly referred to Prof. Dr. H.J. van Zuthem, Macht en Moraal in Arbeidsverhoudingen, Van Gorcum Assen/ Amsterdam 1978.
4   Manders, March 2019.
5   Manders, March 2019.
6   Manders, March 2019.
7   Interview with Freek van Bedaf, February 18, 2019.
8   Strieder, March 2019.

9   See: en.wikipedia.org/wiki/Dot-com_bubble; en.wikipedia.org/wiki/World_Online — both accessed February 4, 2020.

10   Manders, January 2020; Strieder, March 2019.

11   en.wikipedia.org/wiki/September_11_attacks, en.wikipedia.org/wiki/War_in_Afghanistan_(2001%E2%80%93present) — accessed February 9, 2020.

12   en.wikipedia.org/wiki/Early_2000s_recession, en.wikipedia.org/wiki/MCI_Inc.#Bankruptcy — accessed February 9, 2020.

13   Manders, January 2020.

14   Manders, January 2020; Strieder, March 2019.

15   Manders, January 2020.

2   THE RACING STABLE

1   TNO annual report 2018 (income 2018), https://view.publitas.com/cfreport/tno-annual-report-2018_eng/page/26; *Architectenweb*, January 7, 2005 (staff before reorganization 2005), via https://architectenweb.nl/nieuws/artikel.aspx?ID=4175 — accessed February 23, 2020. Herman Wijffels was CEO of Rabobank between 1986 and 1999.

2   Interview with Jan Mengelers, March 20, 2019.

3   Interview with Mengelers.

4   Career data derived from LinkedIn profiles — accessed February 2020

5   Interview with Manders, Jan 28, 2020.

6   Conversation with Manders, March 9, 2020.

7   Interview with Katja Pahnke, February 18, 2019; interview with Mengelers.

8   Business cells at the end of 2006: annual report 2007. Interview with Pahnke. Profile Pahnke on website Eindhoven University of Technology: www.tue.nl/en/storage/staff/katja-pahnke — accessed March 8, 2020.

9   NRC Handelsblad, March 25, 2008. BSO was an acronym for Bureau voor Systeem Ontwikkeling; in English: Bureau for Systems Development.

10   E. Wintzen, *Eckart's Notes* (Rotterdam, 2007).

11   P. van Amelsvoort, B. Seinen, H. Kommers, G. Scholtes, *Zelfsturende Teams — Ontwerpen, invoeren en begeleiden* (2003, revised edition), pp. 10–11.

12   Van Amelsvoort et al., p. 18.

13   Van Amelsvoort et al., pp. 14–15.

14   R. Semler, *Maverick, The Success Story Behind the World's Most Unusual Workplace* (New York, 1993); https://bit.ly/2VCts3E and https://bit.ly/38k6ykf — accessed March 3, 2020.

15   T. Andreoli and E. de Vos, Met koninklijke aanbeveling, in: De Groene Amsterdammer, November 12, 2014.

16   De Groene Amsterdammer, November 12, 2014.

17   De Groene Amsterdammer, November 12, 2014.

18   D. Maister, *Management van professionele organisaties* (Schoonhoven, 1999), pp. 192–194.

19   M. Weggeman & C. Hoedemakers, *Managing Professionals? Don't!* (Amsterdam, 2015).

20   Weggeman (2007).

21   https://bit.ly/32QHBMi — accessed November 3, 2019.

22   The Semco Style Institute website, https://semcostyle.org/programs — accessed February 25, 2020.

23   A. Droste, *Semco in de polder* (Amsterdam, 2007).

24   https://bit.ly/38kVVh4 — accessed January 10, 2020.

25   TMC, Triple Project Memorandum (TPM), December 2018 p. 49

26   TPM, p. 5.

27   TPM, p. 49. These were the business cells in TPM December 2018 (p. 19): Technology Executives, Application Lifecycle Management, Chemical, Civil Engineering, Data Science, Electronics, Field Service, High Tech Systems, Industrial Automation, Life Sciences, Manufacturing Support, Mechanical, Mechatronics, Nanotechnology, New Product Introduction, Physics, Software, Test & Integration.

28   Van Amelsvoort et al., p. 25.

29   Interview with Manders 2020; press release TMC, July 16, 2007.

30   Interview with Manders 2020.

31   ASML annual report 2009, Form 20-F, as deposited with the United States Securities and Exchange Commission (SEC).

32   Interview with Manders 2020.

33   TMC annual reports 2009 and 2011; 2009 derived from 2009 half-year report and press release of March 23, 2010, accessed on www.prnewswire.com/nl/persberichten/tmc-group-verstevigt-fundament-voor-verdere-groei-152512715.html — March 11, 2020.

34   TMC Assessment & Development: annual report 2007 and info from Pontes website — consulted March 10, 2020.

35   TMC 2009 half-year report.

36 TMC annual report 2011; interview with Manders 2020. Business cells in 2009: TMC Automotive, TMC Industrial Automation, TMC Chemical, TMC Embedded, TMC Physics, TMC SAP Professionals, Adapté Bouwkunde & Civiele Techniek

37 Extra dividend: press release March 22, 2011, accessed on https://prn.to/2Ud9ie6 — March 16, 2020. Origin of expression 'fingers in our nose': https://schrijf.be/nl/blog/met-de-vingers-in-de-neus — accessed March 16, 2020. Annual report 2011.

38 Altran interim report 2011. Interview with Manders 2020. Take-over 2019: https://en.wikipedia.org/wiki/Altran#Takeover_by_Capgemini — accessed March 16, 2020.

39 https://nl.wikipedia.org/wiki/Alternext — accessed March 17, 2020. Interview with Manders 2020.

40 The non-executive directors were Jan Lobbezoo, a former CFO of Philips Semiconductors; Hans Wouters, former general manager of Samas Group (a wholesale trading company); and Paul Schouwenaar, former CEO and president of Zeeman Group (a clothing retail chain). Hardly any debt: annual report 2011. Construction Gilde deal: VEB (*Vereniging van Effectenbezitters*, a Dutch Association of Stock Owners), November 12, 2012 — accessed March 17, 2020 from www.veb.net/artikel/04252/oud-oprichters-tmc-toucheren-miljoenen-na-overname.

3 TRANSPARENCY, THAT'S THE DISRUPTIVE THING

1   This report is based on an interview by Beatrix Broekmans, held in September 2019, and Stohr's resume.

2   This report is based on an interview by Beatrix Broekmans, held in September 2019, and Venema's resume.

3   Venema resume. Closure Philips Handheld Diagnostics: *Eindhovens Dagblad*, September 1, 2017: https://bit.ly/2QJazsB — accessed March 24, 2020.

4   Report Broekmans and Anteryon website — March 24, 2020.

5   Report by researcher Beatrix Broekmans.

6   Interview with Pahnke.

7   Interview with Pahnke.

8   Interview by Beatrix Broekmans, September 2019.

9   Report by researcher Krijn Schramade.

10 Report by Krijn Schramade.

11 Interview by Beatrix Broekmans, October 2019.

12   Interview with Robinson, February 18, 2019.

13   Interview with Robinson.

14   TPM, p. 86.

15   Interview by Beatrix Broekmans, October 2019.

16   TPM, pp. 6, 42, 53–54.

17   Report by Marcel Metze.

18   Meeting with Manders and Weggeman, September 9, 2020.

4   THE PILOTS

1   Interview with Venema.

2   Interview with Stohr.

3   Interview with Ignacio Vazquez, August 16, 2019, by Beatrix Broek-
     mans.

4   Interview with Van Leuken.

5   Interviews with Van Bedaf and Van Leuken.

6   Interview with Ronald Cornelissen, February 28, 2019. Océ: nl.wiki-
     pedia.org/wiki/océ. Nedstack: https://nedstack.com/sites/default/
     files/2019-07/nedstack_company_brochure_2018.pdf.

7   Stijn Huijbers worked for TMC from 2011–2015. Then in 2017 he
     co-founded IKONS, a marketing and communications consultancy, with
     TMC's Thijs Manders as a co-investor. In 2018, he joined Waes, a
     recruitment agency specializing in bringing foreign engineers to Europe.
     Source: Stijn Huijbers' LinkedIn profile, Eindhovens Dagblad January 9,
     2017. Push-belt, see https://bit.ly/2SSQ9OJ.

8   Interview with Van Dijke, September 2019.

9   Interview with Van Leuken.

10   A. Bandura, *Social Learning and Personality Development*, New York:
     Holt, Rinehart, and Winston, 1963. J. Rotter, *Social Learning and Clini-
     cal Psychology*, New York: Prentice-Hall, 1954. B. Skinner, *The Behavior
     of Organisms: An Experimental Analysis*, Cambridge, Massachusetts,
     1938.

11   V. Vroom, *Work and Motivation* (revised edition), San Francisco: Jossey
     Bass, 1995. L. Porter and E. Lawler, *Managerial Attitude and Perfor-
     mance*, Homowoxi III: Richard D. Irwin, 1968. J. Kotter, V. Faux & Ch.
     McArthur, *Self-Assessment and Career Development*, Englewood Cliffs
     N.J.: Prentice Hall, 1978. J. Kotter, *Organization: Text, Cases, and
     Readings on the Management of Organizational Design and Change*
     Homewood, III: R. D. Irwin, 1979. S. Covey, *The 7 Habits of Highly*

Effective People: Powerful Lessons in Personal Change, New York: Free Press, 1989. M. Buckingham & D. Clifton, *Now, Discover Your Strengths*, New York: The Free Press, 2001. Ch. Handy, *The Age of Unreason*, Cambridge, Mass: Harvard Business. School Press, 1989. F. Luthans, C. Youssef and B. Avolio, *Psychological Capital*, Oxford University Press, 2007.

12 Source: Pontes bureau presentation 2016 (internal document, provided by Freek van Bedaf); LinkedIn profiles of the respective people.

13 Pontes bureau presentation 2016.

14 Van Bedaf interview.

15 The paragraphs about the assessment procedure are derived from a Pontes bureau presentation 2016.

16 The paragraphs about the reality check are derived from a Pontes bureau presentation 2016.

17 Pontes Group employs around seventy coaches, forty of whom are active in coaching TMC employeneurs, account managers, cell directors and support managers — in the Netherlands and abroad. Pontes also offers assessment and coaching services to other companies. The group wants to spread the employeneurship concept to other companies and sectors as well. For that purpose, it has developed a Q learning branch (to help companies introduce employeneurship, a Q Academy (for training coaches) and Q care (a psychotherapeutic branch). The interview was done by Beatrix Broekmans at the end of December 2019.

5 GOING ABROAD

1 First interview with Emmanuel Mottrie, by the author, February 18, 2019.

2 Interview with Mottrie 1.

3 Interview with Mottrie 1; interview with Manders 2.

4 Interview with Mottrie 1.

5 Interview with Mottrie 1 and Triple Memorandum 2018.

6 Interview with Jaskaran Sandhu, by the author, via Skype, November 6, 2019.

7 Follow-up interview with Emmanuel Mottrie, September 10, 2020.

8 Interview with Loïc le Mené, by the author, via Skype, November 7, 2019.

9 Safran S.A. is a French multinational group, active in aviation, aerospace and defense. The group was formed in 2005 through a merger of

Snecma (aviation) and Sagem (defense). In 2016 it had around 57,500 employees (of whom 60 percent in France), €15 billion in revenue and €2 billion in profit. The main activity is the production of jet engines. Source: https://nl.wikipedia.org/wiki/Safran 20 Jan 2020.

10 Altran Technologies, SA is a global innovation and engineering consulting firm founded in 1982 in France by Alexis Kniazeff and Hubert Martigny. Altran operates primarily in the high technology and innovation consultancy sector, which accounts for nearly 75 percent of its turnover. Administrative and information consultancies account for 20 percent of its turnover with strategy and management consultancies making up the rest. The firm is active in most engineering domains, particularly electronics and IT. In 2018, Altran generated €2.916 billion in revenue and employed over 46,693 people around the world. Source: https:// en.wikipedia.org/wiki/Altran — Jan 20, 2020.
Founded in 1988, ALTEN is a French multinational technology consulting and engineering company with offices in 25 countries. In 2018, ALTEN had 33,700 employees and reported revenue of €2.2 billion. The French market accounts for 45 percent of the group's activity. Source: https://en.wikipedia.org/wiki/ALTEN — Jan 20, 2020

11 Interview with Åsa Åhlander, by the author, via Skype, November 14, 2019. The Swedish å is pronounced like the eu in employeneur, so Åsa becomes eu-sah)

12 Experis is part of ManpowerGroup and specializes in attracting, assessing and placing specialized expertise in the ICT, finance, human resources, engineering and life science sectors. It operates in over fifty countries and deploys more than 38,000 skilled professionals every day. Source: www.experis.be — June 3, 2020.

6   THE CLIENT

1   Infineon: https://en.wikipedia.org/wiki/Infineon_Technologies — viewed June 7, 2020. Interview with Marijn van Os, March 18, 2019. Van Os left Innoluce on September 30, 2020 to become CEO of Scinvivo, a company he founded in 2016. Scinvivo is developing an imaging catheter which will allow a urologist to look inside bladder tissue. The catheter will use optical coherence tomography (OCT) to provide cross-sectional images of the tissue. Source: www.scinvivo.com — viewed June 8, 2020.

2 www.infineon.com/cms/en/about-infineon/press/press-releases/2016/INFATV201610-002.html — viewed June 7, 2020.

3 See for example: www.daimler.com/innovation/case/autonomous/high-way-pilot-2.html — viewed June 7, 2020.

4 Ibid.

5 Results from Bosch, DAF, TNO and Vanderlande interviews in PowerPoint presentations, internal TMC documents, 2017–2018.

6 https://en.wikipedia.org/wiki/Fred_Reichheld — viewed June 7, 2020.

7 Interview with Sietske van Schagen, November 12, 2019, via Skype

8 TMC deployment at ASML number: second interview with Emmanuel Mottrie, March 9, 2020.

9 Interview with Strieder.

10 Manders interview 1; Mottrie interview 2 (numbers decline placements at ASML).

11 Source: TMC 2018–2020 financials, internal document provided by CFO Rogier van Beek.

12 Manders interview 2.

13 Manders interview 2. On April 23, 2018, Emmanuel Mottrie, until then CEO of TMC International became the CEO of the entire TMC Group. At the same date, Thijs Manders became executive president of the group.

14 Interview with Mottrie 2; TMC 2018–2020 financials, internal document provided by CFO Rogier van Beek. Additional information by Mottrie September 7, 2020.

15 TMC 2018–2020 financials, internal document provided by CFO Rogier van Beek.

16 Interview with Rogier van Beek, June 4, 2020.

17 LinkedIn page Ronald van Gerwen, viewed June 15, 2020.

7 THE FUTURE

1 Interview with Van Beek.

2 Interview with Mottrie 2.

3 Triple Memorandum 2018.

4 Based on Triple Memorandum 2018.

5 Interview with Mottrie 2.

6 Triple Memorandum 2018.

7 Interview with Mottrie 2.

8   Triple Memorandum 2018; TMC financials, internal document; interview with Mottrie 2.
9   TMC financials, internal document.
10 Triple Memorandum 2018.
11 Interview with Mottrie 2.
12 Interview with Mottrie 2.
13 TMC Fundamentals Program, November 12, 2019; interview with Mottrie 2 plus additional information from Mottrie, September 2020. Prenella Patterson left the company in 2020.
14 Jonathan Petit profile LinkedIn — viewed June 22, 2020; interview with Mottrie 2.
15 Interview with Mottrie 2.
16 Triple Memorandum 2018; interview with Mottrie 2.
17 Interview with Mottrie 2.
18 Interview with Van Beek.
19 Online interview with Van Beek and Mottrie, September 10, 2020.
20 Additional information from Rogier van Beek, provided September 7, 2020.
21 Van Beek interview June and September, and additional information, September 7, 2020.
22 Van Beek interview June 2020.
23 Ibid.
24 Interview with Marjolein Berkers and Lotte Geertsen, November 13, 2019.
25 Addition: comment by Lotte Geertsen, July 21, 2020.

SOURCES

Annual reports

- Altran, annual report 2008, interim report 2011
- ASML, 2009
- TMC annual reports 2007, 2009 (interim) and 2011

Internal documents

- Pontes bureau presentation. Pontes Group 2016
- Time acquisition, annual report 2018 (final draft)
- TMC client feedback 2017–2018
- TMC, Triple Memorandum 2018
- TMC 2018–2020 financials
- TNO annual report 2018

Literature/further reading

- P. van Amelsvoort, B. Seinen, H. Kommers, G. Scholtes, *Zelf-sturende Teams — Ontwerpen, invoeren en begeleiden* (2003, self-published, revised edition).
- A. Bandura, *Social Learning and Personality Development*. New York, 1963.
- M. Buckingham & D. Clifton, *Now, Discover Your Strengths*. New York, 2001.
- S. Covey: *The 7 Habits of Highly Effective People: Powerful Lessons in Personal Change*. New York, 1989.
- A. Droste, *Semco in de polder*. Amsterdam, 2007.

- E. Goldratt, *The Goal: A Process of Ongoing Improvement*. Pretoria, 1984.
- Ch. Handy, *The Age of Unreason*. Cambridge, Mass., 1989.
- J. Kotter, V. Faux & Ch. McArthur, *Self-Assessment and Career Development*. Englewood Cliffs N.J., 1978.
- J. Kotter, *Organization: Text, Cases, and Readings on the Management of Organizational Design and Change*. Homewood, Ill, 1979.
- F. Luthans, C. Youssef and B. Avolio, *Psychological Capital*. Oxford, 2007.
- D. Maister, *Managing the Professional Service Firm*. New York, 1997.
- L. Porter and E. Lawler, *Managerial Attitude and Performance*. Homowoxi, III, 1968.
- F. Reichheld, *The Loyalty Effect*. Cambridge, Mass., 1996.
- F. Reichheld, *The Ultimate Question 2.0*. Cambridge, Mass., 2011.
- J. Rotter, *Social Learning and Clinical Psychology*. New York, 1954.
- R. Semler, *Maverick, The Success Story Behind the World's Most Unusual Workplace*. New York, 1993.
- B. Skinner, *The Behavior of Organisms: An Experimental Analysis*. Cambridge, Mass., 1938.
- V. Vroom, *Work and Motivation*. San Francisco, 1995.
- A. Watts, *The Wisdom of Insecurity: A Message for an Age of Insecurity*. New York, 1951.
- M. Weggeman & C. Hoedemakers, *Managing professionals? Don't!* Amsterdam, 2015.
- E. Wintzen, *Eckart's Notes*. Rotterdam, 2007.
- H. van Zuthem, *Macht en Moraal in Arbeidsverhoudingen*. Amsterdam, 1978.

Interviews

- Åsa Åhlander (TMC Sweden)
- Freek van Bedaf (Pontes Group)
- Rogier van Beek (TMC CFO)
- Marjolein Berkers (TMC)
- Ronald Cornelissen (TMC)
- Casper van Dijke (TMC)
- Lotte Geertsen (TMC)
- Danny Hameeteman (TMC)
- Linda van Leuken (TMC)

- Thijs Manders (TMC founder and executive president)
- Loïc le Mené (TMC Paris)
- Jan Mengelers (Eindhoven University of Technology, formerly TNO)
- Emmanuel Mottrie (TMC CEO)
- Marijn van Os (Innoluce)
- Katja Pahnke (Eindhoven Engine, formerly TMC, formerly TNO)
- Prenella Patterson (TMC New York)
- Mark Robinson (TMC)
- Jaskaran Sandhu (TMC Belgium)
- Sietske van Schagen (Bosch Transmission Technology)
- Bert Stohr (TMC)
- Hans Strieder (ASML)
- Ignacio Vazquez (TMC)
- Bernardus Venema (TMC)
- Anette Wijnands (Pontes Group)

Reports

- Hackathon Care, November 9, 2019
- TMC Chemical cell Q3 meeting, 8 October 2020
- TMC Fundamentals, November 12, 2019
- TMC introduction (new employeneurs), December 6, 2019
- TMC Manufacturing Support cell, pizza session, October 30, 2019

Scan the QR code below to access TMC videos on YouTube

INDEX

Printed in Great Britain
by Amazon

42817579R00116